NEW TECHNIQUES OF PERSUASION

UNDER THE ADVISORY EDITORSHIP OF J. JEFFERY AUER

HARPER
& ROW
PUBLISHERS

New York
Evanston
San Francisco
London

Gerald R. Miller
Michigan State University

Michael Burgoon
West Virginia University

new techniques
of persuasion

NEW TECHNIQUES OF PERSUASION
Copyright © 1973 by Gerald R. Miller & Michael Burgoon.
Printed in the United States of America. All rights reserved. No part of this book may be used or reproduced
in any manner whatsoever without written permission except in the case of brief quotations embodied in critical
articles and reviews. For information address Harper &
Row, Publishers, Inc., 10 East 53rd Street, New York,
N.Y. 10022.

Standard Book Number: 06-041047-7
Library of Congress Catalog Card Number: 72-7359

CONTENTS

PREFACE

We believe this little book usefully serves several audiences. As a supplementary text in basic courses in persuasion and human communication, it synthesizes a body of theory and research to which the beginning student has not typically been exposed— theory and research that we deem useful for the fledgling practitioner of persuasion. This same synthetic function recommends the volume for those undergraduate and graduate students seeking an introduction to the research conducted in such areas as inducing resistance to persuasion, the persuasive impact of role playing, and the uses and limitations of counterattitudinal advocacy as a persuasive technique. The extensive list of references enhances the book's utility, not only for students of human communication, but also for readers in social psychology, sociology, and other behavioral disciplines.

Like all such undertakings, the finished product reflects the contributions of many persons other than the authors. David K. Berlo, former Chairman of the Department of Communication at Michigan State University, was instrumental in creating an intellectual climate that made it possible for us to share and refine our ideas. Several of our contemporaries at Michigan State University shared with us a lively interest in the research areas covered in the book. In particular, we would like to acknowledge inputs of Edward Bodaken, Frank Millar, Bonita Perry, and Eugene Tate. Finally, the editorial staff of Harper & Row has provided valuable advice and counsel throughout the preparation of the volume. We thank all these people, as well as others, for adding to the strength of the volume, while at the same time assuming sole responsibility for any remaining weaknesses.

GERALD R. MILLER
MICHAEL BURGOON

A FRAMEWORK FOR VIEWING THE PERSUASION PROCESS

To entitle a book *New Techniques of Persuasion* may strike many readers as presumptuous at best, and misleading at worst. For more than 2000 years people have been fascinated with the techniques man uses to influence the actions and attitudes of his fellow men. Countless pages have been devoted to descriptive and prescriptive statements about the persuasion process. Courses in rhetorical theory and criticism, persuasion, and argumentation center on the theory and practice of persuasive communication. Given this long-standing, pervasive interest in persuasion, a skeptical reader has every reason to ask whether there is likely to be anything new under the sun.

Still, after considerable deliberation, we have chosen to retain the adjective "new" in the title of this volume. Moreover, we are willing to offer a cautious defense for so doing. Sticklers for precise usage may argue that the phrase "relatively unexplored" would have produced a more accurate title. Although we would have no quarrel with this substitution, our aversion to lengthy modifiers led to our preference for the word "new," particularly since we do not believe its usage is unduly cavalier.

In the following pages, we explore some dimensions of the persuasion process and some techniques of persuasion previously subjected to relatively limited scrutiny, at least by students of human communication. In this sense, then, these dimensions and techniques are "new," even though practitioners of the art of persuasion may have been employing them for some time. Most of the theoretical and research literature alluded to has accumulated in the past several decades. The lion's share of this literature is attributable to scholars from fields such as social psychology and sociology; however, its relevance to the theory and practice of persuasive discourse should be readily apparent.

Our major aim in this chapter is to provide a framework for dealing with these new techniques of persuasion. To accomplish this end, it would seem to be useful to sketch both a conceptual view and an operational view of the persuasion process.

a conceptual view of the persuasion process

Although current students of persuasion differ on some aspects of their conceptual treatments of the persuasive process, their positions also share numerous common elements. Bettinghaus (1968) defines a persuasive communication situation as one involving "a conscious attempt by one individual to change the behavior of another individual or group of individuals through the transmission of some message" (p. 13). Central to Bettinghaus's definition are the notions of *conscious intent, behavioral change,* and *message transmission.*

Brembeck and Howell (1952) view persuasion as "the conscious attempt to modify thought and action by manipulating the motives of men toward predetermined ends" (p. 24). Like Bettinghaus, these authors stress the *conscious intent* of the persuader. They differ from Bettinghaus, however, in their emphasis on the manipulation of *motives* (motivational constructs are usually viewed as intervening variables; that is, events occurring inside the individual), rather than overt behavior. Moreover, although the book of Brembeck and Howell does devote considerable attention to persuasive message strategies, the authors do not believe that *message transmission* by the persuader is a necessary condition for labeling an influence attempt "persuasion."

Cronkhite (1969) asserts that "persuasion will refer to the act of manipulating symbols so as to produce changes in the evaluative or approach-avoidance behavior of those who interpret the symbols" (p. 15). Unlike the previous conceptual definitions, Cronkhite's does not specify *conscious intent*. Still, the term *manipulation* seems to imply intent, and Cronkhite's analyses consistently focus on situations where intent is an ingredient. Like Bettinghaus, Cronkhite stresses *behavior*, rather than *motives* or *attitudes*, and his emphasis on symbol manipulation by the persuader aligns him with Bettinghaus in viewing *message transmission* as a necessary condition for persuasion.

Scheidel (1967) calls persuasive speaking "that activity in which speaker and listener are conjoined and in which the speaker consciously attempts to influence the behavior of the listener by transmitting audible and visible symbolic cues" (p. 1). His definition expresses concern for *conscious intent, behavioral influence,* and *message transmission.* It is of somewhat more limited scope than the other three conceptual definitions, since it deals with "persuasive speaking," rather than the more generic "persuasion."

The four preceding definitions, although certainly not exhaustive, offer a sample of ways of conceptualizing the process of persuasion. Perhaps the conceptualization of persuasion undergirding this book can best be established by comparing and contrasting it with these treatments, as well as by amplifying some of the implications of the four definitions. Moreover, such an approach permits us to identify the new techniques of persuasion that are of central concern for this book.

We share these contemporary authors' bias that the term "persuasion" should be reserved for situations involving conscious intent on the part of one party (the persuader) to influence another (the persuadee). Our reasons for using the term "persuader," rather than such terms as "source," "speaker," or "communicator" will become apparent as we proceed. Limiting persuasion to situations involving conscious attempts at influence creates certain problems; in particular, it raises the question of how one determines whether intent is present in a particular situation. Even so, there are common-sense grounds for asserting that, in the vast majority of instances, assessment of intent does not pose serious difficulties.

Most observers would concur that when a soap company pays thousands of dollars for a thirty-second spot on network television, it is motivated by a conscious intent to influence the soap-buying behavior of the American public. Conversely, if one or two suggestible students ape the wardrobe of an esteemed professor, it is unlikely that observers would conclude that the professor consciously sought to influence the sartorial preferences of his pupils. Thus debate about intent is limited to those few, unusual situations falling in the twilight zone between conscious intent and unintentional prestige suggestion—a limitation we are willing to accept.

Conceptually, we also agree that persuasive situations involve attempts to influence others. Whether the influence attempt aims at changes in attitudes, motives, values, or behaviors is regarded here as a relatively unimportant problem, perhaps a pseudo-problem. Our lack of concern about the question results from the behavioristic framework that guides our analysis of the persuasion process. All the persuader ever has available to gauge his relative success or failure is the *behavior* of the intended persuadee. True, the persuader may, on the basis of behavioral observations, infer that he has influenced the attitudes, motives, or values of the persuadee. But it is clear that such statements about these intervening processes must result from inferential leaps based on the observation of the persuadee's behavior.

This point can best be illustrated by an example. Suppose a persuader consciously seeks to induce a persuadee to respond in specific ways to the question of whether one should smoke cigarettes. If the persuadee is a smoker, and if after the influence attempt we observe that the persuadee has ceased to smoke, we may conclude that the persuader has succeeded in altering the persuadee's behavior. Suppose, however, we know that before the influence attempt the persuadee consistently said, "I approve of cigarette smoking," but that after the attempt he began to assert, "I disapprove of cigarette smoking." In such a case, we would probably say that the persuadee has changed his attitude about cigarette smoking.

Actually, however, the positing of persuadee attitude change is an inference based on a change in his verbal behaviors concerning cigarettes—for after all, verbalizing, like smoking, involves a sequence of behaviors. Moreover, if the persuadee said he disapproved of smoking but still continued to smoke, we would be hard pressed to decide whether the influence attempt had changed the persuadee's attitudes. Thus, although the following chapters use both the terms "attitude" and "behavior," we are assuming that any statements about attitude change are grounded in behavioral evidence.

About the phrase "influence attempt," however, a crucial distinction must be made; it pertains to a dimension of persuasion discussed in later chapters. The notion of behavioral influence does not necessarily imply modification or reversal of an overt, nonverbal behavior, nor does it always indicate change in the valence or relative attractiveness of an attitudinal statement. For if a persuadee subscribed to a particular attitude with moderate intensity before an influence attempt but held that same attitude with extreme intensity after receiving the persuader's message, the influence attempt would be viewed as successful: behavior would have been affected even though the persuader sought no change in the valence of the attitude. By the same token, if persuasive inputs cause a persuadee to be more resistant to counterpropaganda (i.e., messages seeking to alter his behavior or change the valence of his attitudes), then the source of those persuasive inputs has been successful.

Rather than aiming at changes in attitudes and behaviors, much persuasive communication seeks to reinforce currently held convictions and to make them more resistant to change. Most Sunday sermons serve this function, as do keynote speeches at political conventions and presidential addresses at meetings of scholarly societies. In such cases, emphasis is on making the persuadees more devout Methodists, more active Democrats, or more committed psychologists, not on converting them to Unitarianism, the Socialist Workers Party, or romance languages.

The value of persuasion as an inhibitor of change

5

is undeniable. Nevertheless, in examining the writings in the field, from antiquity to the present, we find relatively few pages devoted to persuasive techniques that seek to increase resistance to change. Instead, persuasion is treated almost exclusively as a facilitator of change: *persuasion is almost synonymous with changes in overt behavior or attitudinal valence.*

In the previous two decades, a body of research dealing with techniques for inducing resistance to change has accumulated. We view this research as a valuable, largely ignored contribution to the literature of persuasion. Consequently, our conceptual view of the persuasion process specifies two kinds of influence attempts: first, attempts that seek to bring about behavioral reversals or changes in the valence of an attitude; second, attempts that aim at making already existing attitudes and behaviors more resistant to change. Moreover, we think that the literature dealing with the second persuasive objective bears on a new technique of persuasion; consequently, we discuss its implications for the persuasion process in subsequent chapters.

Finally, our conceptual view of the role of symbol manipulation, or message transmission, in the persuasion process goes beyond the one stipulated by most contemporary writers. We agree that a process should not be labeled *persuasive communication* unless behavioral and attitudinal modifications result primarily from the effects of symbolization. We do not, however, deem it necessary for the primary symbolizing agent to be the persuader, and this accounts for our use of the term "persuader," rather than "source" or "speaker." Typically, communication scholars have viewed persuasion as a process in which an active communicator (persuader) strives to do something to a relatively passive audience (persuadees)—to influence attitudes or behaviors by skillful manipulation of symbols.

Much recent research has centered on situations in which the roles of persuader and persuadee are defined quite differently. Rather than encoding messages to relatively passive persuadees, the persuader induces them to encode the messages themselves: in a sense, persuasion occurs because the persuadee acts upon himself, instead of being acted upon by the persuader. It is this active involvement in formulating arguments and constructing messages that causes some writers to label the process *self-persuasion.*

In the following chapters, we consider the implications of theoretical and research literature dealing with two such persuadee-centered techniques of persuasion: the generalized case of role playing as a persuasive strategy and the more limited instance of counterattitudinal advocacy. Both techniques rely on the validity of Pascal's injunction that "We are more easily persuaded, in general, by the reasons we ourselves discover than by those which are given to us by others" (in Elms, 1969, p. iii).

At this juncture, the reader should be able to note where our conceptual viewpoint of the persuasion process coincides with those of other writers and where it departs or extends beyond other conceptualizations. These departures and extensions constitute the central focus of this volume; they are what we have labeled "new techniques" of persuasion. A more precise operational description of our view of the persuasion process should serve as a useful final preliminary to our consideration of these techniques.

---

an operational view of the persuasion process

Operationally, we find it useful to conceive of the persuasion process as one in which the persuader strives to establish particular relationships between his own attitudinal or behavioral states and those of the intended persuadees. By concentrating on the sought-after correspondence between the psychological states of the persuader and the persuadee, rather than on characteristics of the transmitted messages, we can avoid some of the traps that have snared previous writers. For example, emphasis on the attitudinal and behavioral postures of those involved in the persuasive process, rather than on message qualities, permits us to avoid questions about the stylistic and content differences between a given persuasive message and another one that aims at information exchange or conflict resolution. We do not contend that such message differences are non-existent, or even that they are unimportant to potential persuaders, but we do hold that in labeling a communicative transaction *persuasive,* the paramount question concerns the type of relationship the persuader seeks to foster between his own attitudes and behaviors and those of the intended persuadee, not the types of messages encoded.

Figure 1 is an operational description of the relationship most commonly studied by students of persuasion: one in which the persuader strives to reverse a behavior of the persuadee or to change the valence of the persuadee's attitude. Prior to the influence attempt, as Figure 1a indicates, the positions of the persuader and the persuadee do not coincide. For the sake of convenience, the discrepancy is pictured as a continuum; nevertheless, the difference sometimes seems to take the form of a simple dichotomy. For example, the persuader may be a parent concerned about a behavior of his teenage son; he may believe that his son occasionally smokes marijuana and he wants him to stop. In this situation, the initial discrepancy can be described as follows: the persuader (parent) wants the persuadee (son) to refrain completely from smoking marijuana, whereas the son believes that occasional marijuana smoking is acceptable and, in addition, actually smokes pot periodically. A continuum may seem inappropriate here; instead, the outcomes may appear to be two-valued. If the father induces the son to quit smoking marijuana, the parent has been successful; if the son continues to smoke it, the father's persuasive attempt has been unsuccessful.

Examination of Figure 1b, which diagrams several possible postpersuasion positions of the persuadee, suggests that even if a situation involves reversal of a particular persuadee behavior or attitude, a dichotomous "on–off" approach is grossly oversimplified. Ideally the persuader seeks complete conversion; he would like the postpersuasion attitudes or behaviors of the persuadee to coincide with his own. Practically, of course, such psychological correspondence seldom results from a single influence attempt. As Figure 1b illustrates, movement toward the persuader's position short of complete conversion is the more likely outcome of an influence attempt. Thus, although the son may not respond by completely abandoning marijuana, he

8

Figure 1   a / Position of persuader and persuadee prior to influence attempt   b / Several possible persuadee changes following influence attempt

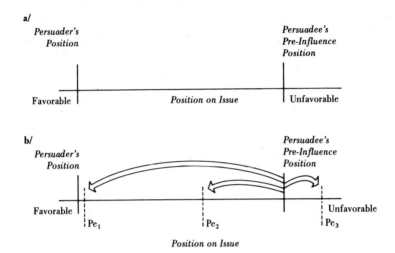

a/

Persuader's
Position

Persuadee's
Pre-Influence
Position

Favorable   *Position on Issue*   Unfavorable

b/

Persuader's
Position

Persuadee's
Pre-Influence
Position

Favorable   Unfavorable

Pe_1 Pe_2 Pe_3

Position on Issue

Pe_1 = change optimally consistent with persuader's intent

Pe_2 = typical change resulting from a single influence attempt

Pe_3 = boomerang effect, persuadee changes counter to persuader's intent

may reduce the frequency of his smoking, or he may start to question the wisdom of such activities, either overtly to others or covertly to himself. Finally, the influence attempt may conceivably backfire completely. Rather than moving toward the persuader's position, the persuadee may move further away from it. In our hypothetical example, the son may rebel and smoke marijuana more frequently following his father's persuasive efforts.

To the extent that such changes can be indexed, we can speak meaningfully of degrees of persuasive success. Moreover, it is possible to systematically study ways in which various persuader, message, channel, persuadee, or context variables influence persuasive outcomes; that is, we can examine ways in which these variables facilitate or inhibit persuadee attitudinal or behavioral change. As we have indicated, this is the kind of situation that has received the major attention of persuasion scholars.

Consider, however, our hypothetical father and son in another attitudinal relationship. As a result of prior influence attempts, the son not only agrees that smoking marijuana is detrimental, he also does not engage in pot smoking. Figure 2a diagrams the initial identity of the persuader's and the persuadee's positions. The father is aware his son is about to begin college and that, upon entering this new environment, he will be exposed to a barrage of counterpropaganda; that is, other potential persuaders will strive to change the son's attitudes and behaviors in the manner illustrated in Figure 1. In this situation, the father's persuasive task is not to reverse an existing behavior nor to alter the valence of an existing attitude, but rather to reinforce already existing attitudes and behaviors, to make them more resistant to change. From the persuader's viewpoint, Figure 2b illustrates the desired post-persuasive relationship between persuader and persuadee attitudes, with the plus sign indicating that the persuadee's attitudes are more strongly held than they were prior to the influence attempt. Of course, as Figure 2b also indicates, the influence attempt may not succeed in strengthening the initially held attitude. If it does not, the persuader has been unsuccessful.

Some readers may hold that the distinction between the two persuasive objectives is unimportant, since the success or failure of the persuader is dependent on the same variables. To argue this way, however, is to beg an important factual question; specifically, are the variables influencing a persuasive attempt to change behavior and attitudes the same as those affecting an attempt to render attitudes and behaviors more resistant to change? Our answer to this question is detailed in Chapter 2, which centers on research relevant to inducing resistance to change. It is sufficient to state now our belief that there are some important differences in the two processes, particularly in the strategies that should be employed to assure maximum persuasive success. Moreover, we believe that serious students of persuasion should be aware of the ways in which resistance can be induced.

In the preceding discussion we have tried to distinguish between a persuasive attempt that aims at

Figure 2   a / Position of persuader and persuadee prior to influence attempt   b / Position of persuadee following a successful influence attempt and an unsuccessful influence attempt

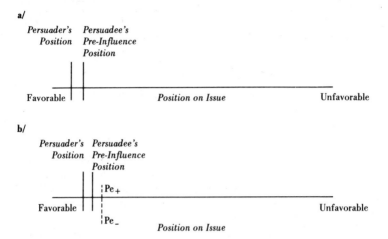

Pe_+ = successful influence attempt, persuadee holds initial attitude with greater intensity

Pe_- = unsuccessful influence attempt, persuadee holds initial attitude with same or less intensity

altering attitudes or behavior—a situation studied extensively by students of persuasion—and an attempt that seeks to make attitudes or behavior more resistant to change—a situation we view as a relatively unexplored dimension of the persuasion process. As indicated earlier, however, we have also chosen to extend our view of the persuasive communication process to situations in which the persuadee, rather than the persuader, is the primary symbolizing agent. This distinction between situations in which the persuader is the primary symbolizing agent and those in which the persuadee assumes the primary symbolizing role can be clarified by an operational description of the two persuasive paradigms.

In the persuasive situation described in Figure 3, which has received careful study by students of persuasion, the persuader is the primary symboliz-

11

Figure 3　A persuasive paradigm in which the persuader is the primary symbolizing agent

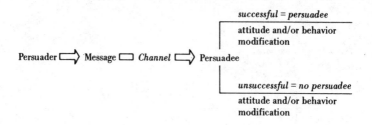

ing agent. After determining his persuasive purpose, the persuader encodes a message and transmits it over some channel to the intended persuadees. They in turn decode and interpret the message: If the persuader has been relatively effective, attitudes or behaviors will be altered or will become more resistant to change; if he has been relatively ineffective, such changes will not occur. Although the persuadee must engage in the cognitive activities of decoding and interpreting the persuasive message, primary symbolizing activities are delegated to the persuader. Speaking of the centrality of this paradigm to scholarship in rhetorical theory and persuasive communication, Miller (1969) asserts:

Central to this view . . . are the terms *active speaker* (persuader) and *relatively passive audience* (persuadees); for even after one pays the customary, contemporary homage to the importance of audience feedback, there still remains no doubt about the locus of major activity, involvement, and energy. It is, of course, by design rather than accident that the only kind of question not requiring an overt answer is a rhetorical question. Nor is it a coincidence that one often hears references to dynamic speakers, but seldom to dynamic audiences. In the traditional rhetorical [persuasive] paradigm, the persuader *acts*, while the persuadee is *acted upon* (p. 2).

Examples of this approach to persuasion abound; indeed, it is perhaps superfluous to develop yet another. Still, for purposes of comparison with the alternative paradigm in which the persuader is not the primary symbolizing agent, let us return to the case of the father and his pot-smoking son. Should the father elect to use the persuasive paradigm just diagrammed and described, he will compose a message consisting of all the arguments he can muster against smoking marijuana. In the typical household, he will sit down with his son some evening and present the message to him. Depending on his own characteristics as well as those of his son, the father may allow intermittent questioning and argument from his son, or he may demand silence.

From the father's viewpoint, his persuasive success or failure hinges on the presence or absence of certain attitudinal and behavioral changes on the part of his son. Unfortunately, we are unaware of any data concerning the frequency of the relative success or failure of this kind of influence attempt, although its use in the family setting is commonplace. Nevertheless, although we do not wish to wear the mantle of pessimists, we suspect that such attempts fail more often than they succeed.

Suppose, however, that our hypothetical father adopts another approach to the influence attempt, one that allows his son (the intended persuadee), rather than himself, to assume the primary symbolizing role. Assume that the father structures the following situation: the son is asked to imagine that he has been arrested for possession or use of marijuana. In accordance with legal procedures, he is permitted to telephone his parents to inform them of his arrest. The father asks the son to role play the telephone call with him, with the father taking his regular role and the son taking the role of a just-arrested teenager.

In his capacity as intended persuader, the father assumes that this role-played communication transaction will modify his son's attitudes toward smoking marijuana. Rather than bombarding his son with reasons for avoiding it, the father places the youth in a hypothetical situation underscoring possible undesirable consequences of his behavior. The aim is persuasive and the success of the influence attempt depends on communication, but there is a drastic change in the symbolizing roles taken by persuader and persuadee. We view such role-playing techniques, when used with persuasive intent, as relatively unexplored, "new" dimensions

Figure 4 A persuasive paradigm in which the persuadee is the primary symbolizing agent (counterattitudinal advocacy paradigm)

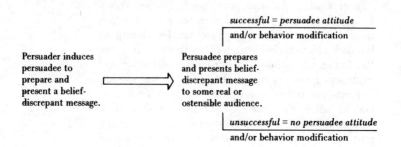

Persuader induces persuadee to prepare and present a belief-discrepant message.

Persuadee prepares and presents belief-discrepant message to some real or ostensible audience.

successful = persuadee attitude and/or behavior modification

unsuccessful = no persuadee attitude and/or behavior modification

of persuasion, dimensions of import to students and practitioners of persuasion.

But, in addition, the last several decades have witnessed the emergence of a considerable body of research dealing with a particular kind of role-playing situation, one in which the intended persuadee is asked to take a position that is demonstrably at odds with his prior beliefs. This persuasive paradigm, described in Figure 4, can best be explained by reverting to our familiar example of father and son. Suppose that instead of asking the son to role play a teenager arrested for marijuana offenses, the father, in his capacity as intended persuader, suggests that the son prepare a message containing all the arguments he can muster against marijuana smoking and that he then present the message to some audience: the father himself, the other members of the family, or a group of teenage peers. From the father's viewpoint, public advocacy of these belief-discrepant views concerning marijuana should cause the son to adopt a less favorable stance toward smoking pot. To the extent that this change occurs, the influence attempt has been successful; to the extent that the son's attitudes and behaviors about marijuana remain unchanged, the father has been unsuccessful in his influence attempt.

There is a marked contrast between the counterattitudinal advocacy paradigm described in Figure

4 and the typically studied persuasive paradigm discussed earlier. As Miller (1969) has indicated, the counterattitudinal advocacy paradigm:

> involves a drastic change in the roles taken by both the persuader and the persuadee. No longer is the persuader the active agent; rather, once the influence attempt has been triggered, he plays a relatively minor part. By contrast, the persuadee is highly involved throughout the influence attempt: *rather than being acted upon, persuasion occurs only if he acts upon himself* (p. 3).

The reader may ask how counterattitudinal advocacy—which is, after all, a form of role playing—differs from the generalized case of role playing discussed earlier. Perhaps the greatest difference results from the degree of specificity with which one can identify the cognitive processes activated in the persuadee, as well as the situational circumstances relating to those cognitive processes. Consider again the two varying situations in which the intended persuader, the father, places the intended persuadee, the son. In the first situation, the son is asked to role play a teenager whose activities have resulted in his arrest, to act "as if" his actions have produced harmful personal outcomes.

Although certain psychological theories and particular research studies suggest that the son's involvement may produce changes in his attitudes and behaviors in respect to marijuana, it is difficult to specify the cognitive processes and activities that produce these changes. Does the son actually identify with the arrested teenager? Does assuming the role create conflict between prior attitudes and public behavior? Does the son experience guilt as a result of his role-played transgressions? Or does some other set of mediating circumstances account for the persuasive impact of the communication transaction? Because of the difficulty in specifying the precise situational factors surrounding the influence attempt, these questions are difficult to answer.

By contrast, the situational factors associated with counterattitudinal advocacy are somewhat more easily specified. At a minimum, we know that the intended persuadee has been placed in a situation where he must publicly encode a message at odds with his prior beliefs; in the typical generalized case of role playing, we cannot be certain that such attitudinal discrepancies actually exist. Moreover, the communication transaction, at least in terms of message preparation and presentation, is somewhat more structured in the counterattitudinal advocacy situation. For these reasons, we deem it useful to deal with the two situations separately, for we hold that they do differ at least in degree, if not in kind. Both, however, are viewed in subsequent chapters as new techniques of persuasion.

summing up

In this chapter we have sought to provide a framework for considering several relatively unexplored, new techniques of persuasion. To accomplish this goal, we have outlined our conceptual and operational views of the persuasion process.

Like several other contemporary writers, we agree that the term "persuasion" should be employed only when there is *conscious intent* on the part of one individual (the persuader) to influence another (the persuadee). Moreover, we share the bias of other writers in holding that persuasive attempts aim at *behavioral influence*, and that influence attempts meriting the label "persuasive communication" must involve *message transmission*. In regard to the latter two criteria, however, we make two crucial distinctions which provide the organizational focus for this volume:

1 / We distinguish between two kinds of behavioral influence. In the first the objective is to bring about the alteration of existing attitudes or behaviors; in the second, the objective is to make existing attitudes and behaviors more resistant to change. The former objective has been extensively studied by students of persuasion; the latter has been relatively unexplored and is, therefore, one of the new persuasive techniques we will consider.

2 / We distinguish between influence attempts in which the primary agent of message transmission or symbolization is the intended persuader, and attempts in which the primary agent is the intended persuadee. The former circumstance has been widely

investigated by students of persuasion; however, little attention has been given to situations in which the major symbolizing agent is the intended persuadee. This volume considers two such general types of situations: one which we label the generalized case of *role playing* and the second which we call *counterattitudinal advocacy*. Each, in our opinion, deserves to be called a new technique of persuasion.

INDUCING RESISTANCE
TO PERSUASION

Our first "new technique of persuasion" centers on making existing attitudes and behaviors more resistant to change. As we stated in the preceding chapter, students of persuasion have devoted much attention to the process of altering existing behaviors or attitudes. Literally hundreds of reported studies suggest combinations of variables that are likely to result in successful persuasion. Most published knowledge claims by persuasion scholars are accounts of the variables operating when someone or some group yielded to a persuasive attack. Another avenue of analysis, largely ignored by students of human communication, is the study of situations in which attitude change did not occur, situations in which people *resisted* the persuasive appeal.

This chapter deals with ways to affect a persuadee's processing of intended persuasive messages so that he does not yield to future persuasive attempts. Research in this area has produced two broad classes of outcomes: 1 / procedures have been suggested to make people generally resistant to persuasive appeals without regard for specific variables such as topic and sources, and 2 / procedures have been suggested to make people more resistant to persuasion in specific situations. This chapter discusses the more generalized procedures

Figure 5   A persuasive paradigm in which the persuader attempts to induce resistance to a future persuasive attack on the persuadee

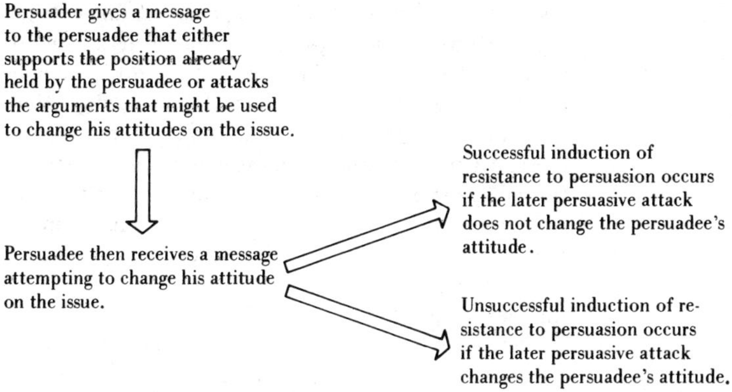

Persuader gives a message to the persuadee that either supports the position already held by the persuadee or attacks the arguments that might be used to change his attitudes on the issue.

Persuadee then receives a message attempting to change his attitude on the issue.

Successful induction of resistance to persuasion occurs if the later persuasive attack does not change the persuadee's attitude.

Unsuccessful induction of resistance to persuasion occurs if the later persuasive attack changes the persuadee's attitude.

first and then turns to research dealing with situationally bound attempts to heighten persuadee resistance.

The general research procedures used to induce resistance to change fit our operational definition of persuasion offered in Chapter 1 and demonstrate why the process of inducing resistance is best viewed as an extension of the persuasion process. In most studies of inducing resistance to change, a persuader transmits to the persuadee messages that are intended to change the persuadee's way of processing later persuasive messages. In simple terms, the persuadee receives a pretreatment message or messages seeking to reduce his vulnerability to subsequent persuasive appeals. If the pretreatment is successful, persons exposed to the pretreatment message demonstrate less attitude change following a later persuasive attack than do persons who do not receive the pretreatment message. (Figure 5 presents a description of this research paradigm.)

To return to our hypothetical parent–child relationship, suppose that the father has two sons who, because of prior persuasive attacks, have become convinced that smoking marijuana is harmful. Moreover, assume that both boys are entering college in the fall and the father fears that persuasive attacks on campus will change their attitudes toward pot smoking. To counteract this possibility, he presents messages to one son designed to make him resistant to the persuasive appeals of his college peers. However, because the second son is out of town for the summer, he does not have the benefit of these resistance treatments. If the claims that resistance to persuasion can be induced are correct, the son who received the messages prior to leaving for college should be more resistant than his brother to any campus messages favoring marijuana smoking. The second son, on the other hand, is more likely to be persuaded to smoke, or at least to believe that smoking marijuana is acceptable.

The rest of this chapter discusses how to plan a persuasive attack designed to induce resistance to later persuasive appeals. We have divided the chapter into five sections. The first deals with individual differences in the persuadee which may affect influenceability; the second examines methods for changing people's internal belief structures so as to alter the ways they process persuasive appeals, and the third discusses the ways people reduce cognitive inconsistency and therefore become more resistant to persuasive attempts. The fourth section of the chapter is devoted to a discussion of what McGuire (1964) has called the inoculation model of resistance. Finally, in the last section, we consider methods of training people to enhance their critical ability and subsequently to increase their resistance to incoming persuasive appeals.

individual persuadee differences

Considerable research conducted within the more traditional persuasion paradigm of changing persuadee attitudes or behaviors has centered on individual difference variables affecting persuasibility. For instance (and this is bound to irritate "liberated" women), the research rather clearly demonstrates that females are more susceptible to persuasive appeals than are males. However, for at least two good reasons, we will not pursue the implications of this research in this section. First, little research performed within the resistance-to-persuasion paradigm has looked at such individual difference variables as age and sex, and second, our publisher indicates that 50 percent of our potential target audience happens to be female. Therefore, we turn our attention to several personality variables that influence people's resistance to persuasion.

SELF-ESTEEM

Several researchers have attempted to manipulate self-esteem in order to learn how changes in that variable influence resistance to persuasion. Early research (Kelman, 1950; Hochbaum, 1954; Samelson, 1957; Stukát, 1958) led to the conclusion that giving a person a success experience prior to a persuasive attempt makes him more resistant to change. Gelfand (1962) demonstrated that the person can be made more resistant to social change even if the success experience is not related to the issue on which social pressure is exerted. Mausner and Bloch (1957) noted that the resistance-inducing effect of a success experience is further enhanced if the persuadee witnesses the simultaneous failure of the person who is later to become the source of the influence attempt. All this research seems to indicate that people who have experienced success become more confident and, in turn, more resistant to social influence. Still, a careful analysis of these studies reveals some problems related to the general applicability of the findings.

Later research and theory suggest that the effects of raising self-esteem are not as simple as the previous research implies. For example, early researchers created rather simple situations of the suggestibility and conformity types in which the persuasive message itself was not a major variable in attitude change. In other words, the messages were simple suggestions or requests; they were not very complex in style or content. Gollob and Dittes (1965) found that message complexity interacts with self-esteem in producing resistance to persuasion. If a person has low self-esteem, raising his self-esteem by exposing him to successful experiences is likely to increase resistance to persuasion. This main-order effect is consistent with earlier research. But raising a person's self-esteem is less likely to increase resistance to persuasion if the persuasive appeal is complex, requiring a considerable amount of cognitive activity to process the information presented, than if the message is simple and requires little cognitive processing.

It appears that raising an individual's self-esteem decreases his persuasibility because he becomes more confident and less vulnerable to persuasive attacks. He also becomes more receptive to messages and does not withdraw from persuasive appeals. In other words, the self-confident person is also more aware of and better able to comprehend persuasive messages. In simple suggestibility or conformity situations (Gelfand, 1962; Gollob & Dittes, 1965), all subjects comprehend the persuasive attempt equally well, so people high in self-esteem (whether natural or induced by success experiences) are the most resistant to persuasion. When the persuasive appeal consists of a complex message, awareness and comprehension assume importance, since increasing self-esteem also increases message receptivity. Thus increases in self-esteem are offset by increased comprehension of the persuasive message, which in turn lowers resistance to persuasion in complex message situations on the part of persuadees who are high in self-esteem.

This reasoning implies that the level of chronic self-esteem does not matter in the simple suggestibility experiments. Since in both experimental and control groups all chronically low self-esteem persons are equally receptive to the simple message, raising self-esteem by way of success (experimental groups only) increases the resistance to persuasion (again, experimental only) and therefore accounts for the early findings. Conversely, when complex messages are presented, those chronically low in self-esteem are more receptive to the message after they have undergone a successful experience and the offsetting effect of greater receptivity makes it difficult to predict degree of resistance to persuasion.

Perhaps a return to our hypothetical father and sons will clarify this important point. Suppose the father wishes to prepare his sons for simple messages that demand conformity from the recipients.

The relative level of self-esteem of the two sons should have little effect on their ability to comprehend the message; consequently, the boy whose self-esteem is raised, say by a successful experience, should show the greater *increase* in resistance to persuasion. But if both boys are low in self-esteem and the messages dealing with marijuana are likely to be complex, the father's choice of strategies is less clear. Suppose he decides to manipulate the first son's self-esteem, raising it by exposing him to successful experiences. This son should gain self-confidence, becoming *more* resistant to persuasion; unfortunately, he should also be more receptive to later persuasive messages and *less* resistant to their persuasive appeals. Thus the poor father doesn't know what effect his manipulation will have.

Furthermore, assume that the other son, also low in self-esteem, is allowed to go to college without any attempt to make him more resistent to persuasion. Being low in self-esteem, he is *not* resistant to change, but being unreceptive to messages, he *is* resistant to persuasive appeals. If both boys were high in self-esteem, the same circumstances would pertain. Any increases in their self-esteem would be offset by their increased awareness; still, the problem would be less critical, since the two boys high in self-esteem would be fairly resistant to change anyway. But in both cases, our manipulative father is damned if he does and damned if he doesn't.

In summary, raising a persuadee's self-esteem is a relatively effective way to induce resistance to simple suggestions or to bold conformity appeals. When the person is being prepared for complex messages requiring a great deal of cognitive processing, the effect of raising self-esteem is complex and does not lend itself to precise predictions about the degree of resistance to persuasion that will be conferred.

HOSTILITY

Other writers interested in inducing resistance to persuasion have suggested that the persuadee's level of hostility may affect resistance to persuasive appeals. They have reasoned that raising a person's level of hostility by annoying or abusive behavior may result in increased resistance to social influence because of the persuadee's general dislike for mankind. A classic study by Weiss and Fine (1956) provides an interesting extension of this line of reasoning. The authors found that when a person is subjected to abusive treatment prior to a persuasive appeal, he becomes more resistant to persuasive appeals arguing benignly but more susceptible to appeals arguing for harsh actions. Thus, although hostility does seem to make a persuadee more negative toward his fellow man, the Weiss and Fine study demonstrates that the topic is an important consideration serving to modify this general conclusion. When a person's internal state causes him to dislike his fellow men, he becomes *more* receptive to appeals derogating man and *less* receptive to messages aimed at good or neutral actions.

Several other studies indicate that among males chronic hostility is associated with resistance to persuasion. This may be one reason for females' being generally more persuasible—they are less hostile in most situations. Certainly, further research on the relationship of level of hostility to subsequent resistance to persuasion is needed. Researchers have previously experienced difficulty in inducing hostility, and no way has been found to manipulate specifically the hostility level of persuadees.

ANXIETY

Another individual difference variable that has received the attention of researchers interested in inducing resistance to persuasion is the persuadee's level of anxiety. As with the other variables we have discussed, the relation between level of anxiety and resistance to persuasion is complex. Nunnally and Bobren (1959) found a direct relation between level of anxiety and resistance to persuasion: people who received a threatening, or anxiety-producing message on a topic were less willing to receive further messages about the issue. Janis and Feshbach (1953) offer results that seemingly contradict this conclusion. They found that the greater the prior anxiety arousal, the less resistant a person becomes to subsequent persuasive attacks.

24

Later research seeks to explain these apparent contradictions by focusing attention on the nature of the fear-arousing message. Millman (1965) suggests that there is an interaction between the chronic anxiety level of the persuadee and the number of irrelevant fear appeals in the persuasive message. She reported that for persons generally low in anxiety, the inclusion of irrelevant fear appeals decreased resistance to persuasion. Conversely, for chronically anxious people, the use of irrelevant fear appeals increased resistance to subsequent persuasive messages.

As was found in the research on self-esteem, the complexity of the persuasive appeal seems to interact with the persuadee's anxiety level in producing resistance to persuasion. Millman (1965) suggests that complex messages, which necessitate considerable cognitive processing by the persuadee, require low fear appeals for optimal attitude change. Her suggestion is consistent with the reasoning that increases in such factors as self-esteem or anxiety lead to greater resistance to persuasion *except* in situations where increased receptivity to complex messages offsets this effect.

However, findings of a study by Singer (1965) reveal a trend that conflicts with the previously discussed research. Singer found that the optimal level of fear arousal was higher for less intelligent than for highly intelligent people. Those aroused most (high fear, low intelligence) were least resistant to the persuasive message. Even though the highly intelligent persons were probably more receptive to the complex messages and might thus be expected to exhibit more attitude change, Singer concluded that the greater the prior anxiety arousal, the less resistant a person will be to persuasive appeals.

In general, we agree with McGuire's (1969) conclusion that frightening a person (even on irrelevant issues) can have one of two effects: it tends to increase resistance to persuasion when the person is chronically high in anxiety and to lower resistance when the person is chronically low. We also suggest that when dealing with complex persuasive appeals, the interactive effects of increased arousal and increased comprehension of the message make predictions about subsequent resistance to persuasion difficult.

EDUCATION

Another individual difference variable among persuadees that has received limited attention is education. Available research indicates that the nature of the persuasive appeal is critical in specifying the effect of education or intelligence on resistance to persuasion. Stukát (1958) and Crutchfield (1955) found that more intelligent individuals demonstrate greater resistance to social pressure from peers. Conversely, some research (Ward & Wackman, 1971) suggests that more intelligent people are less resistant to persuasive attempts emanating from the mass media. Given these results, along with the previously discussed findings of Singer on fear appeals and intelligence, we are forced to conclude that intelligence alone is not a good predictor of resistance to persuasion. More research is needed to specify what, if anything, intelligence interacts with in creating resistance to persuasion.

A final note about the utility of individual difference variables in arriving at strategies for inducing resistance to persuasion seems to be appropriate. In research settings, such variables as self-esteem, anxiety, and hostility can be dealt with in at least two ways. The investigator may seek to manipulate the variables situationally (i.e., he may provide the person with successful or unsuccessful experiences, say threatening or demeaning things to him, etc.), or he may attempt to assess "the amount" of the variable that is normally carried around by the person (i.e., he may administer a generalized paper-and-pencil test of self-esteem, anxiety, or hostility). The first approach we will label *situational*, the second *manifest*, or *chronic*.

A persuader who aims at making others more resistant to persuasion frequently finds it difficult if not impossible to assess the chronic level of a persuadee's self-esteem, anxiety, or hostility—it is seldom feasible to administer paper-and-pencil inventories to one's intended persuadees. Of course, if the persuader knows the persuadee well, some predictions are possible. Thus our hypothetical father could probably make a fairly accurate assessment of either son's chronic self-esteem, anxiety, or hostility. But if the same man's intended persuadees were an audience of relative strangers, he would probably be hard-pressed to predict the chronic level of one of these variables. This suggests that the utility to the persuasion practitioner of research findings growing out of the chronic approach is limited at best.

---

changing internal belief structures

One of the most popular explanations of attitude change is derived from a family of psychological theories labeled *cognitive consistency* theories. Such cognitive consistency theories as cognitive dissonance (Festinger, 1957) are discussed in detail in Chapter 4. For the moment, we indicate simply that an assumption central to all consistency theories is that the individual tries to keep his internal beliefs, his verbal statements, and his other overt behaviors in agreement. Needless to say, the average person does not always accomplish this goal; still it is assumed that people are ever motivated to achieve cognitive balance.

The notion of cognitive consistency can be illustrated by harkening once again to the situation in which our hypothetical father finds himself. Presently, his son's beliefs, attitudes, and behaviors regarding pot smoking are in harmony; his cognitive house is in order. Shortly, however, the son is likely to be exposed to persuasive appeals calculated to induce cognitive inconsistency—namely, appeals stressing the merits of marijuana. Since inconsistency is psychologically discomfiting, the son will be motivated to behave in ways intended to restore equilibrium. One possible choice is to modify his original position about the use of marijuana and to become more favorable toward it. A second alternative is to resist the appeals of the pro-marijuana message by denying their validity or by derogating the message source. The father, of course, hopes that his son will choose the latter means of reducing inconsistency.

One variable that often determines the way chosen to restore consistency is commitment. Mc-Guire (1969) suggests that a person's belief should become more resistant to change if he becomes more committed to the belief. The person can become committed by thinking about the belief and in turn believing more intensely in his position, by making a verbal statement and becoming publicly identified with the belief, or by acting overtly in some way to irreversibly identify himself with a given belief. Since changing a belief creates inconsistency among earlier thoughts, verbal statements, and overt behaviors, the more committed a person is to a position, the less likely he is to yield to a persuasive attack.

Early theorists such as Lewin (1951, 1958, 1965) predicted that anything which induces people to come to a private, unstated position commits them to the position and makes subsequent persuasive appeals less successful. Although Lewin predicted that public commitment would further freeze individuals' beliefs against persuasive appeals, Bennett (1955) demonstrated that public commitment was no more effective than private decision making in conferring resistance to persuasion. Work by Fisher, Rubinstein, and Freeman (1956) provides only indirect support for the notion that public commitment increases resistance to subsequent persuasive appeals. In their study, individuals learned to carefully avoid committing themselves publicly on discrepant beliefs and were therefore resistant to persuasive attempts.

In general, prior research supports the notion that increasing commitment to a belief increases resistance to subsequent persuasive appeals. In particular, the evidence clearly demonstrates that forcing a person to publicly commit himself to a belief is an effective way of increasing resistance to subsequent persuasive appeals. If our hypothetical father can induce his son to utter public indictments against pot smoking, he enhances the possibility that the son will resist pro-marijuana appeals originating from his college classmates.

But it is possible to go beyond public verbal

endorsement of a belief, to induce persons to engage in other overt behaviors consistent with their beliefs. Kiesler (1968, 1971) provides the most comprehensive summary of research dealing with the relation between publicly behaving in a manner calculated to reinforce a private belief and subsequent resistance to persuasive attempts. The dynamics of inducing resistance to persuasion by involving people in public acts that reinforce their private beliefs are probably similar to the more direct persuasive impact of the role playing and counterattitudinal advocacy situations described in the following chapters. McGuire (1969) points out that the research indicates that the conditions under which active participation occurs determine the magnitude of subsequent commitment. Generally speaking, if the overt behavior is performed under conditions of little pressure, reward, or justification, a person shows more resistance to subsequent attacks than if he actively defends his position under considerable pressure or for a large reward. Even so, we advise postponing acceptance of this generalization *in toto* until Chapters 3, 4, and 5 have been read; this material deals with variables affecting persuasion in role playing and counterattitudinal advocacy situations.

Although we personally agree with McGuire's statement, several competing theoretical positions do not hold that low pressure for commitment activities leads to greater resistance to persuasion. As Kiesler and Sakumura's (1966) summary suggests, there are so many variables interacting with justification, reward, and choice that sweeping generalizations concerning the effects of these variables on commitment are probably impossible.

A final form of commitment has been called external commitment; it involves telling a potential persuadee that a third party thinks that he holds a certain belief. The persuadee is then presented with a message attacking the position attributed to him. Persons who are immunized against persuasion by this pretreatment technique are more resistant to attacking messages than persons who have not been externally committed (Rosenbaum & Franc, 1960; Rosenbaum & Zimmerman, 1959). Papageorgis (1967) explains these findings by suggesting that commitment plays a less important part in con-

Table 1 The levels of commitment

Level	Method of Achieving
1/ Private belief	Minimum requirement for resistance to future persuasion. Anything that forces a person to make a private decision.
2/ Public endorsement	Forcing people to publicly endorse a belief.
3/ Behavioral commitment	People commit an irreversible behavior, e.g., signing a statement supporting a belief.
4/ External commitment	Telling a person someone else believes he holds a certain position.

ferring resistance to persuasion than does the consensual validation of the first position. Regardless of how one interprets these findings, they demonstrate that the method of telling someone that others believe he holds a certain position is an effective method of creating resistance to persuasion.

Table 1 summarizes the levels of commitment we have discussed. These levels can be illustrated by referring again to our hypothetical example. If the son is to resist future pro-marijuana messages, the minimum requirement is that he privately believe pot smoking to be harmful. As we indicated earlier, the father may increase his son's resistance to future persuasive messages by inducing him to utter public endorsements of this belief (the second level of commitment summarized in the Table). Moving to the third level, the father may encourage his son to become a counselor in a drug rehabilitation center or to become involved with a young people's group campaigning against the use of marijuana. In this case, the father, in his role as persuader, assumes that his son's behavioral commitments will further heighten his resistance to subsequent persuasive appeals emphasizing the desirable aspects of smoking marijuana. Finally, at the fourth level, the father may occasionally remind his son of others who know of the son's negative views about marijuana; his persuasive strategy may center on external commitment of his son. In some cases, the father may combine all four commitment levels, on the assumption that using them all will make the youth maximally resistant to persuasion.

ANCHORING

Let us turn to another resistance-inducing technique derived from consistency theory, the technique of *anchoring*. The theory underlying this technique rests on the assumed need of a person to remain consistent. Whereas the commitment technique just discussed assumes a desired consistency among private beliefs, public pronouncements, and overt behavior, anchoring approaches attempt to induce resistance to persuasion by linking one belief to other beliefs that a person holds. This approach assumes that if one belief is tied to another belief, either by creating links between them or by making existing links appear to be more important, resistance to subsequent persuasive appeals will result. When two beliefs become anchored (linked in some manner), a person must change both beliefs or experience cognitive inconsistency. Since changing two or more beliefs is more difficult than changing a single belief, successful anchoring creates more resistance to persuasion.

McGuire (1969) suggests methods for inducing resistance by linking beliefs to: 1 / accepted values or goals, 2 / related beliefs on other issues, and 3 / liked individuals or groups. The remainder of this section discusses methods for creating these anchors.

Accepted Values and/or Goals Assuming that persons often hold a belief because it apparently facilitates goal achievement, resistance to persuasion can be created in two ways. Prior to a persuasive attack, the relevant goal can be made perceptually salient (i.e., the persuadee can be reminded of the goal and of its importance to him), thereby reducing the chances of a successful attack. A less difficult task might be to demonstrate the necessity of holding a belief if a particular goal is to be achieved. For example, managers of business organizations sometimes use this persuasive technique to combat union activity. Suppose an employee has

31

a goal of keeping his job and earning a living wage. Managers might try to link the belief that they want to foster (unions are bad) to the antithesis of the goal (that the union will cause the company to shut down, causing jobs to be lost). To the extent that management is successful, the employee will be resistant to the persuasive campaign of the union. In this situation, as in many everyday cases, it is difficult to alter the persuadee's perception of the goal. It is hard to imagine a communication strategy that seeks to increase a person's desire to earn a living wage. A more feasible strategy is to link the belief about the advisability of unionization to the goal of remaining employed. Management should link unionization to closing the plant or rejecting the union to continued employment.

When an individual actively establishes the link between beliefs and values, he becomes even more resistant to change (Nelson, 1966). In our example, management might use the immunization strategy of giving cost data to employees and allowing them to discover the link between the union and eventual close-down. Participating in this discovery should make the employee even more antiunion than if management had asked him to receive passively the company's persuasive appeal.

Linking to Related Beliefs on Other Issues As we previously stated, the more firmly related beliefs are anchored, the more resistant a person becomes to persuasive attacks. Abelson and Rosenberg (1958) posited that a person has cognitive links between issues about which he holds beliefs. Moreover, in line with consistency theories, they assumed that the person strives to maintain a coherent, internally consistent set of positions on these issues. They asked people to examine beliefs and to decide if a given belief was consistent with others. This technique was designed to induce resistance by demonstrating to a person the degree of inconsistency he would face if he changed a single belief.

There is, however, a potential danger associated with the procedure. When linking a belief to other beliefs, the persuader runs the risk of all related beliefs changing when a given belief is successfully attacked. Consider once more our hypothetical father and son. The son presently believes "Marijuana is bad," and this belief is linked to such beliefs as "The government is truthful and it says marijuana is bad," "The Justice Department justly prosecutes violators of the law," and "My father believes marijuana is bad, and I respect his views." If a college acquaintance persuades the son to try marijuana and if the son finds it has no apparent bad effect, he will not only change his attitude toward marijuana, he will also change his beliefs about the government and about his father. As he changes these other anchored beliefs, a general antagonism toward all institutions and authority figures may result. This "multiplier" effect can lead to general states of alienation and rebellion. So we must point out that although anchoring generates resistance to persuasion, there is a danger that many related attitudes will rapidly change if one firmly anchored belief is successfully attacked.

Linking to Individuals or Groups Linking a person's beliefs to his relationships with other individuals or groups can induce resistance to later persuasive appeals. There are several techniques for conferring resistance in this way. Suppose a persuader demonstrates the linkage of a particular belief to a person by saying to an intended persuadee, "Since you believe in x, person Y likes you." If the persuadee values the opinion of person Y, he will think that believing *not-x* will result in psychological discomfort. His apparent alternatives are to end his relationship with Y or to change Y's beliefs. Realizing the difficulty involved in trying to effect either alternative, he becomes more resistant to persuasive messages advocating *not-x*.

Research (Bennett, 1955) indicates that a link with anonymous individuals or groups can bring resistance to persuasion. In other words, the persuadee does not even have to know personally the referenced individual or group to value his shared beliefs with them. Journalists often refer to "reliable sources" or "high officials." Such allusions should have the effect of immunizing people against attacks on the journalist's position. Students speak of the beliefs of "other college students" and appear reluctant to change attitudes that are linked to these often anonymous individuals.

33

Resistance can also be created by reinforcing and strengthening established links. We can raise the positive feelings a person always has toward some individual or group and thereby make him resistant to persuasive attacks. For example, if our hypothetical son becomes a fraternity member and if he has positive feelings toward the group, the dean of students may stress to the son the group's public stance against drug use. By emphasizing the importance of the group and their attitudes, the dean may make the son more resistant to pro-drug appeals.

methods of reducing cognitive inconsistency

The preceding section has explained how persuaders can use manipulations to create cognitive inconsistency in persuadees, thus making them more resistant to later persuasive appeals. This section deals more precisely with the reduction of *existing* inconsistency, and it explores ways in which reduction of inconsistency can create resistance to persuasion.

Congruity theory (Osgood & Tannenbaum, 1955) postulates that attitude change occurs because of perceived discrepancies between sources and attitude issues. For example, when a highly valued source makes a negative assertion about something or someone perceived favorably by a person, incongruity results. Figure 6 demonstrates this state of incongruity. If individual A feels positively about both the attitude issue and the source of a negative assertion about that issue, he must do something to make the situation more congruous. If a person who abhors the war in Viet Nam hears Bob Hope, whom he enjoys as a performer, speak in favor of involvement in Southeast Asia, he has two alternatives for establishing cognitive consistency: he can become less positive toward Bob Hope or he can become more favorable toward American involvement in Viet Nam. Much of the research suggests that attitudes toward issues are less resistant to change than are attitudes toward sources. Still, there are techniques that a persuader can use to increase the pressure to change source attitudes and

Figure 6   A paradigm in which incongruity exists because of perceived discrepancies between sources and attitude issues

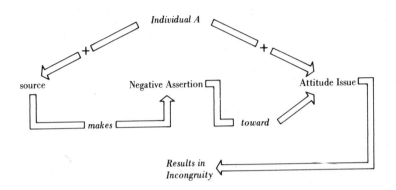

to decrease the pressure to change issue attitudes. Let us consider two of these techniques.

SOURCE DEROGATION

One way to make the attitude issue more resistant to persuasive attacks is to lower the credibility of the source of negative or positive assertions about the issue. For example, a persuader might attack the message source prior to having the intended persuadee hear an assertion about the attitude issue in question. This technique is often used in courtroom situations. If a defense attorney can successfully derogate a prosecution witness before the witness has given his damaging testimony, the jury can be made resistant to the prosecution's persuasive appeals.

DENIAL

The attitude issue can also be protected from persuasive attack by having the source deny any responsibility for assertions about the attitude issue. In other words, if someone has successfully linked a source with an attitude issue, a persuader could attempt to destroy that link and to establish resistance on his side of the attitude issue. It should be noted, however, that Tannenbaum, Macaulay, and

Norris (1966) found that mere source denial of any connection with the assertion does not prevent attitude change. Macaulay (1965) demonstrated that, if the persuadee is to be made more resistant to later persuasive attacks, the source must first deny any incongruent assertion and then make an assertion congruent with the persuadee's position. In other words, merely breaking an established anchor will not confer resistance; a new link must be established that strengthens the denial of the source–assertion incongruity.

Tannenbaum has worked with types of messages needed to reduce source–assertion incongruity, but discussion of these message treatment techniques is deferred until the next section of this chapter, which deals with specific techniques for "inoculating" individuals against persuasive attacks.

message strategies to "inoculate"

McGuire's (1964) inoculation approach to conferring resistance to persuasion draws on a biological analogy. Just as a person is immunized by pre-exposing him to weakened doses of a disease, so can a persuader immunize persuadees against future appeals. McGuire's procedure requires messages that will stimulate defenses but not destroy them, so that a person becomes resistant to later persuasive attacks. The research discussed in this section has been divided into two separate message strategies designed to immunize persons against persuasive appeals: 1 / the use of supportive message pretreatments (i.e., evidence that either further supports or induces an individual to gain information supporting his present beliefs), and 2 / the use of refutational pretreatments (i.e., statements attacking appeals that are counter to the person's beliefs). Thus, as the time draws short for his son's departure to college, our hypothetical father may bombard the youth with further arguments and information reinforcing his anti-marijuana views (supportive defense), or he may anticipate some of the pro-marijuana arguments his son will encounter at college and then go on to point out the weaknesses of these arguments (refutational defense).

Congruity theory (Osgood & Tannenbaum, 1955; Tannenbaum, 1956) posits that the more intense an attitude, the more resistant it is to persuasive attack. If this is correct, one way of immunizing people against persuasive appeals is to strengthen the intensity of attitudes already held. As we stated in Chapter 1, this technique of persuasion is worthy of more research and study than it has received. Attempts by Tannenbaum et al. (1966) to strengthen initial attitude positions by giving a pretreatment message containing evidence supporting an individual's belief demonstrate the utility of such a strategy.

McGuire and Papageorgis (1961) argue, however, that this supportive technique of strengthening attitudes is relatively ineffective in producing resistance to persuasion because it does not follow the defense-alerting model discussed earlier. They claim that presenting supportive arguments and evidence does not motivate the persuadee to acquire additional information and hence does not prepare him for later persuasive attacks. In their frequently cited study, McGuire and Papageorgis found no differences in resistance between a group given a supportive pretreatment message followed by a persuasive attack and a group exposed only to the persuasive attack. Although attitudes appeared to be strengthened immediately following the pretreatment message, this strengthening produced little resistance to the subsequent attack.

Examination of the studies by Tannenbaum et al. and by McGuire and Papageorgis suggests that the contradictory findings may have resulted from differing research procedures. The Tannenbaum et al. study attributed the pretreatment message to a source labeled a "professional committee," and the McGuire and Papageorgis study presented the message without attributing it to a specific source. As we indicated earlier, linking of beliefs with sources, even anonymous groups or individuals, creates resistance to persuasion. It is possible that this source-pretreatment anchoring yielded additional resistance in the experiment of Tannenbaum et al. and, when considered in conjunction with other findings, their results imply that supportive

37

pretreatment messages are more effective when attributed to a source.

McGuire has conducted additional research that confirms his contention that implied threat is a necessary element to induce resistance to change. McGuire and Papageorgis (1962) found that warning people of a persuasive attack—or, as they put it, threatening them with the possibility of a future attack—is more effective than a supportive pretreatment alone. The combination of the threat of having to deal with the attack along with the supportive message induced more resistance than the message alone. Moreover, threat in the form of refutational messages (i.e., appeals attacking counterarguments) can also be used effectively in conjunction with supportive messages.

McGuire (1961) and Tannenbaum and Norris (1965) both demonstrated that combining supportive and refutational messages was more effective than presenting supportive pretreatments alone. McGuire claims that refutational messages are threatening and account for the resistance when combined with supportive evidence. Tannenbaum disagrees, alleging that the refutational messages merely add new defense material to the supportive material, thus strengthening existing attitudes.

Researchers (McGuire & Papageorgis, 1961; McGuire, 1962, 1964) have also sought to determine if active participation in creating supportive messages leads to more enduring resistance than does passive reception of previously prepared supportive messages. These researchers reasoned that creating supportive messages is perhaps too demanding a task for unprepared persuadees, who are likely to have little knowledge about the attitude issue. Still, even though the task is highly demanding, it should also be motivating for the persuadee. Initially, because of the difficulty of the task, participation should interfere with defense mechanisms, since the persuadee does not have an ample opportunity to consider the arguments. If this is true, passive reception of prepared messages should lead to more immediate resistance to persuasion, and indeed, findings support this prediction.

Since participation is more motivating and since no information is immediately presented to subjects in the participation condition, it should take more time for people to build defenses to repel persuasive attacks. Moreover, such active participation should produce greater long-term resistance. Consistent with this likelihood, McGuire finds that resistance conferred by passive message reception decays similar to a forgetting curve, whereas those who engage in active participation grow more resistant to change with time. Thus, if our hypothetical father seeks short-term resistance, he should provide his son with prepared supportive arguments; if he wishes to increase the probability of long-range resistance, he should involve the son in the construction of supportive messages.

In summary, McGuire has provided considerable evidence to support his inoculation theory. The efficacy of using only supportive messages presented for passive reception is certainly questionable. Even so, other researchers have made contributions suggesting useful linkages of supportive messages and sources and providing evidence for the immediate resistance conferred by supportive defense strategies. In the following section, we examine more closely the use of refutational message strategies to confer resistance to persuasion.

REFUTATIONAL PRETREATMENTS

When using the refutational pretreatment technique, arguments are presented which attack the persuadee's beliefs; then these arguments are rebutted. McGuire (1969) and Tannenbaum (1966) attest to the success of this method in conferring resistance to attitude change; in fact, this problem area is one of few in the persuasion literature that has produced successful replications of findings. At the same time, there is some disagreement about the theoretical reasons for the findings.

McGuire posits two reasons for the success of the refutational technique: threat and provided defense. When the arguments on the other side of the issue are mentioned, a person realizes that his belief is threatened and he becomes motivated to defend the belief; in addition, the rebuttals provide a defense which the motivated person accepts.

There is considerable research evidence to support McGuire's position. We mentioned earlier the relative superiority of supportive and refutational arguments to supportive messages alone. In addition, McGuire and Papageorgis (1961) demonstrated that refutational defenses containing arguments different from those appearing in the subsequent attack induced as much resistance as pretreatments giving attacks and rebuttals for the identical arguments presented in the subsequent attack. This finding supports McGuire's contentions that the threat of refutational messages is necessary and that the subjects prepared themselves for any attack, rather than merely rehearsing specific arguments and leaving themselves defenseless against new arguments. This evidence, in addition to the prewarning studies mentioned earlier (i.e., studies in which the persuadee is told that one of his beliefs will subsequently be attacked), implies that threat is a very important part of resistance conferred by refutational message strategies.

Still, threat alone does not appear to be effective in producing resistance to persuasion; people must have the chance to establish adequate defenses if they are to withstand a persuasive attack successfully. As we mentioned earlier, if people are exposed to a persuasive attack immediately following a supportive pretreatment message, giving them the arguments is superior to allowing them to create their own.

McGuire has shown that this temporal effect is influenced according to whether the refutational arguments are the same as or different from those contained in the persuasive attack. When the arguments in the refutational pretreatment are different, passive reception is no longer superior to active participation. Since the person can only have defenses for issues refuted in the pretreatment messages, a new set of arguments in the persuasive attack leaves him defenseless. Thus, as was the case for persuadees who create their own messages, people who face different appeals in the attack need time to create adequate defenses. When the same arguments are given in a pretreatment message and in a subsequent persuasive attack, those persons *given* refutational arguments are more resistant than either persons *given* supportive arguments or persons allowed to *create* their own defenses. When time is allowed between pretreatment and attack, individuals who actively create their own arguments become increasingly more resistant to persuasion over time.

As a whole, the preceding research supports McGuire's theoretical position that optimum resistance requires both threat and available refutational positions. Tannenbaum et al. (1966) explain the effectiveness of the refutational model in a somewhat different manner. They posit two other mechanisms that make the refutational message strategy work: "assertion weakening" (refutation) and "concept boosting" (support). To test this position, Tannenbaum and Norris (1965) attempted to assess the effects of four variables discussed earlier in this chapter. Specifically, they created experiments that combined source derogation, denial, supportive pretreatments, and refutational pretreatments in various ways. As we have said, source derogation and denial are useful ways to reduce source–assertion incongruity, whereas the two message strategies do not aim at inconsistency reduction. In all cases, refutational message strategies contributed more to conferring resistance than did source derogation or denial. The results also indicated that supportive and refutational message strategies have little to do with congruity theory predictions.

Tannenbaum (1966) has devised yet another explanation for resistance to persuasion resulting from refutation. Based on the assumption that the more intense the source's assertion, the more the pressure for attitude change, Tannenbaum claims that it is possible to weaken the assertion by refuting points in the attack. This treatment is identical to McGuire's refutation strategy with the addition of sources, but the theoretical explanation is somewhat different.

Although there are many research data linking negative and positive sources to a variety of assertions, we think that the evidence indicates that effects of the source manipulations are so minimal that congruity theory is rendered less useful. According to the earlier research, the effects of supportive and refutational pretreatments seem to explain a major part of resistance to attitude change. Kelman and Hovland's (1953) finding that source and assertion are disassociated over time, thus minimizing the source's importance, leads us to conclude that researchers would be wise to give up on Tannenbaum's search for the proper source-assertion combinations and to concentrate on refining the refutational and supportive message strategies.

Briefly, the important inoculation research findings are as follows: refutational message strategies tend to be more effective than supportive messages initially, and they also provide longer lasting resistance to persuasive attacks. The resistance conferred by active participation is less than that provided by passive message reception, but it is more enduring. Although much effort has been expended to specify the effects of source–assertion interactions, the characteristics of the message appear to be much more important than source characteristics in conferring resistance.

training in critical ability

The previous sections of this chapter have dealt with research techniques of two kinds: those which center on motivating the persuadee, as with such individual difference variables as self-esteem or anxiety, and those which create specific types of messages, as with supportive or refutational defense strategies. Our approach may have provided little comfort for the student of persuasion who would appreciate practical suggestions to implement research findings. Although our discussion has focused on behavioral approaches to inducing resistance to persuasion, it seems that the time-honored approach of developing skills in critical ability is a useful way to put the research to use.

Most of the investigations by behavioral scientists have indicated that pretraining in critical ability slightly enhances a person's capacity to resist persuasion, but the improvement is disappointingly minimal. Studies by McGuire and Tannenbaum show that people can be trained to be critical on specific issues but that attempting to confer generalized resistance by training in broad critical techniques is only marginally successful. This inability to train people to be generally resistant to persuasive attacks deserves attention by those involved in the field of human communication, which for centuries has offered courses in criticism and in argumentation as applied logic. McGuire (1969) points to pedagogical issues worthy of careful consideration. First, he claims that the behavioral scientists cannot specify the proper techniques of criticism for evaluating persuasive messages. Moreover, if the techniques of criticism required to confer general resistance to persuasion were known, it still might be difficult to teach them.

Also there have been "boomerang" effects when critical training has been attempted. Sometimes, when people are told the intent of a persuasive message, the message actually becomes more rather than less persuasive. Training in analyzing and evaluating arguments may increase the person's awareness of and attentiveness to the arguments, thus making the individual more persuasible rather than more resistant. Also, if people are trained to accept some arguments and to discount others, another kind of "sleeper effect" may operate over time—just as people disassociate sources from messages as time passes, so might discounted arguments be forgotten and only the persuasive arguments be remembered.

These problems and possibilities should be of interest to teachers, critics, and behavioral scientists concerned with persuasive communication. The persuasion literature has long been filled with "offensive game plans" that tell how to change a person, regardless of whether the change is good for him. It seems to us that in a time marked by a veritable explosion of persuasive communication, people need added resources to defend themselves against the barrage of persuasive attacks they face daily. Indeed, students of persuasion need to spend as much time and energy on the study of persuasive consumption as they have devoted to the study of persuasive production in the past.

---

summing up

In this chapter we have discussed numerous strategies that may be employed to induce resistance to persuasion. Some of these strategies lend themselves to particular issues and problems; others serve as models for inducing generalized resistance. In choosing among the various strategies, a persuasion practitioner will find it necessary to analyze his own persuasive needs for a given situation.

Students interested in persuasion research cannot help but note how little is known about resistance-generating strategies. We hope that future research will fill in some of the gaps and provide at least partial answers to some of the theoretical enigmas posed in this chapter.

ROLE PLAYING AS A
PERSUASIVE TECHNIQUE

Imagine yourself as a patient waiting anxiously in a doctor's office. The doctor enters, a grave expression on his face, and seats himself behind his desk. He speaks:

"Well, last time you were here you asked for the whole truth, so I'm going to give it to you. This X-ray (pointing to it) shows there is a small, malignant mass on your right lung. Moreover, results of the sputum test confirm this diagnosis."

"What you're saying, doctor, is that I have lung cancer, right?"

"Unfortunately, the tests leave no doubt about the diagnosis."

"What next?"

"Immediate surgery is necessary. I've arranged for you to report to the hospital tomorrow morning. Plan on spending at least six weeks there, because chest surgery requires a long convalescence."

"I dread asking this question, but how are my chances?"

"I wish I could be totally encouraging; however, frankness dictates that I tell you there is only a moderate chance for a successful outcome from surgery for this condition."

"It there anything I can do to improve my chances?"

"We've discussed this before, but I'd like you to refresh my memory on your smoking habits."

"I suppose you'd call me a fairly heavy smoker. I've been smoking almost two packs daily for the last four years."

"It is urgent for you to stop smoking immediately, since every cigarette aggravates your condition. Moreover, I know you're quite anxious about the news I've just given you, and this itself will make it harder to stop. Therefore, we should spend some time right now discussing the difficulties you expect to encounter in quitting smoking."

"Well, first . . ."

Undoubtedly, similar conversations take place daily in doctors' offices throughout the country. The preceding dialogue, however, is patterned after a role-playing sequence used in several previous studies (Janis & Mann, 1965; Mann, 1967; Keutzer, Lichtenstein, & Himes, 1969). The question of concern to these researchers was whether active involvement in such an emotional scene would produce changes in the role players' smoking habits. In other words, they sought to determine if emotional role playing is a viable persuasive technique.

Before considering these researchers' conclusions, let us examine some of the characteristics of the situation in which the role player, who is also the intended persuadee, finds himself. First, he is asked to behave "as if" he is faced with certain circumstances; he literally becomes an actor. To the best of our knowledge, none of the subjects in any of the prior studies actually had lung cancer. Still, the situation is not highly implausible, particularly since all the subjects were moderate to heavy smokers. So although there is an illusion of the stage associated with the performance, there is also an aura of reality calculated to produce a powerful emotional impact on the role player. It actually could happen to him!

Second, as we noted in Chapter 1, if attitudes are altered by such role taking, it may be difficult to specify the reasons for the change. For instance, if persons who are asked to assume the role of a lung cancer victim subsequently quit smoking, the action may be attributed to health-related anxiety they experienced while playing the role, guilt or shame they felt about their own smoking, their covert or overt rehearsal of antismoking arguments, or yet some other mediating factor.

Finally, when viewed as a persuasive transaction, the active involvement of the intended persuadee is apparent. Rather than passively attending to antismoking arguments, the persuadee is drawn into dialogue; he is forced to verbalize his anxieties, to discuss courses of action open to him, and to ponder the consequences of his behavior. In short, his symbolization is at least as important as the symbolization of the persuader.

Does active involvement in role playing modify existing attitudes? Results of the Janis and Mann (1965) study indicate that it does. When compared with control subjects who did not role play but rather listened to the information contained on a taped role-playing session, subjects who actively role played exhibited the following behavior: 1 / they became significantly more convinced that smoking causes lung cancer, 2 / they expressed significantly greater fear of personal harm resulting from smoking, 3 / they indicated significantly greater willingness to try to modify their smoking habits, 4 / they professed a significantly firmer intent to quit smoking immediately and, two weeks later, 5 / they reported a significantly greater decrease in the number of cigarettes smoked daily.

In explaining the persuasive efficacy of the role-playing experience, Janis and Mann assert that "During the performance unpleasant outcomes such as pain, physical incapacity, hospitalization and death seem to acquire in fantasy a personal reality that is usually resisted when people are told about these same threatening outcomes in the usual types of warning communications" (pp. 89–90). If their analysis is accurate, it underscores the importance of the persuadee's active involvement in the influence process.

Nor do these changes in smoking behavior appear to be short-lived; in fact, evidence indicates that they persisted over a lengthy time period. Mann and Janis (1968) report results of two follow-up interviews of control and role-playing subjects, one conducted about eight months after the original experiment and the second conducted approximately 18 months after the study. In both interviews, role players reported significantly lower daily consumption of cigarettes than did their control counterparts. The Surgeon General's original report on the harmful effects of smoking was released during this time period, but it did not appear to be a crucial determinant of smoking decisions. As one subject put it:

The [Surgeon General's] report did not have much effect on me. But I was in this other study. A professor was doing this psychological thing and I was one of the volunteers. And that was what really affected me. . . . He was the one that scared me, not the report. . . . I got to thinking, what if it were really true and I had to go home and tell everyone that I had cancer. And right then I decided I would not go through this again, and if there were any way of preventing it I would. And I stopped smoking. It was really the professor's study that made me quit (p. 342).

Such testimony underscores the powerful persuasive impact of the role-playing experience.

Earlier we suggested that it may be difficult to specify why role playing is an efficacious persuasive technique. Mann (1967) attempted to deal with this problem by comparing the effects of three role-playing situations: a situation based on fear, a situation based on shame, and a cognitive role-playing situation. The three conditions can best be contrasted by describing the situation the subject was asked to imagine:

(Fear group) Imagine that I am a doctor and you are my patient, and here in the doctor's office I actually tell you that smoking has seriously harmed your health. [Note that this situation is identical to the one used in the study of Janis and Mann.]

(Shame group) Imagine that I am a doctor and you are my patient, and here in the doctor's office I actually tell you that smoking shows your lack of self-control and sets a bad example to others.

(Cognitive group) Imagine that I am the coach of the debating team and you are a debater, and we are preparing for a debate in which you must argue that people should stop smoking (p. 338). [This situation is similar to the counterattitudinal advocacy paradigm pictured in Chapter 1 and discussed in Chapters 4 and 5.]

Generally, results indicated that the fear role-playing experience produced greater change in smoking attitudes than did cognitive role playing. The fear and shame conditions did not differ significantly. In addition, male subjects who engaged in a high level of verbalization (i.e., who became highly involved in the role play) demonstrated greater attitude change in the fear and shame conditions than did male subjects whose verbalization level was low. Conversely, highly verbal females in the shame condition resented the entire exercise, and under these circumstances, a boomerang effect occurred (i.e., the subjects actually became more adamant about their smoking habits). These differences between levels of verbalization and between male and female subjects underscore the complexity of some of the relationships dealt with in Mann's study.

We have described the several studies of Janis and Mann rather thoroughly, for we feel that they offer dramatic evidence that role playing can have a powerful persuasive impact. To be sure, our enthusiasm is tempered by several considerations. A later study by Keutzer, Lichtenstein, and Himes (1969) found no persuasive effect among the role-playing subjects, although these authors suggest that the female smokers in their study may have been more cognizant of the health peril associated with smoking than were Janis and Mann's subjects, since the Surgeon General's report was released prior to the study of Keutzer et al. Certainly, if people continue to smoke in the face of warnings about potential health hazards, it is likely to be difficult to change their smoking habits by means of any persuasive technique.

Perhaps a somewhat more important consideration is that attempts to change attitudes through role playing have centered entirely on the issue of cigarette smoking. Janis and Mann admit that this issue may be particularly suited to the emotional dynamics of the role-playing experience. Undoubtedly studies dealing with other issues are needed to assess the general effectiveness of this persuasive technique. It would, for instance, be interesting to place teenagers in a situation where they are being interrogated by the police after arrest on a drug charge and then to determine whether this role-playing experience affects their attitudes toward use of marijuana.

If the preceding evidence constituted the sum of our knowledge about the persuasive efficacy of role playing, the topic would probably not merit a chapter in this book. But role playing has been used in other persuasive arenas. In particular, the technique has been employed in psychotherapeutic settings where the purpose is to foster personal growth and development of a better self-concept. We turn next to an examination of this persuasive dimension of the role-playing technique.

role playing as an instrument for developing attitudes toward self

Most frequently, we think of persuasion as a process intended to alter or reinforce people's attitudes about aspects of the external world; in fact, our examples and illustrations have thus far focused on this objective. A father tries to influence his son's attitudes about the use of marijuana. A researcher tests a persuasive technique by using the question of cigarette smoking and its effects on health. An employer strives to inculcate certain employee attitudes about unionization. In each case, the persuader's purpose is to foster certain persuadee perceptions of aspects of the external world and to ensure that the persuadees will behave consistently with these perceptions.

But people also have perceptions of themselves. Sometimes the persuader's object is to change these perceptions, these attitudes toward self. Our hypothetical father may decide (even though as we indicated in the preceding chapter, such a determination is difficult to make) that his son's self-esteem is so low that he is an easy mark for persuasive messages stressing the virtues of pot smoking. Rather than instituting a barrage of additional anti-marijuana communications, the father may try to persuade the son to have a higher opinion of himself; he may try to bring about an increase in the son's self-esteem. In this particular instance, such a persuasive goal may be only a means toward the end of making the son more resistant to pro-marijuana appeals. Often, however, this is not the case, for a persuader may seek to change a persuadee's attitudes toward self solely on the grounds that such changes will make the persuadee a happier, more functional individual.

The division between the external world and the self does not imply that the two realms are mutually exclusive. Obviously, the experiences we have with our external environment shape our attitudes toward self. Conversely, our self-perceptions influence our interactions with that environment. If a person is consistently rejected by others, he develops an unfavorable self-concept; in turn, his unfavorable self-concept causes him to avoid contacts with others. Still, if we wish to induce him to engage in more human commerce, we may decide that the most effective strategy is to persuade him to perceive himself more favorably, rather than beseiging him with messages about the joys of human companionship. Such a strategy assigns higher immediate priority to self-attitudes, while viewing attitudes toward the external world as secondary.

The preceding circumstances are often present in therapeutic settings. Although some therapists may bridle at our position, we deem it reasonable to assign to the therapist the role of persuader and to designate the client as the persuadee. Certainly, such role prescriptions are in keeping with the conceptual and operational views of persuasion set forth in Chapter 1. Moreover, the therapist may employ various persuasive strategies to bring about favorable changes in client self-attitudes. One persuasive strategy frequently employed is that of role playing.

Consider, for example, the psychodrama, a therapeutic technique fathered by J. L. Moreno:

Psychodrama consists of two roots—drama means action; and psycho meaning mind. It is really mind in action. In a way we can say that a psychodramatic session is like life in its highest potential. Life, as you are living it, with the one difference that all the inner forces that you have are coming out. The psychodrama is, therefore, a vehicle by means of which life itself is lived under the most favorable and most intensive kind of circumstances (1957, p. 281).

The scenario for a psychodrama is usually rooted in the external world; however, the persuasive intent of the therapist is to modify client attitudes and feelings toward self. Moreno describes a situation in which a husband died suddenly and was buried while his wife was away. Upon her return, the wife had difficulty adjusting to her new circumstances. Undoubtedly she felt guilty about her absence, and this guilt, combined with her loneliness, caused her to feel that she too had died but had not experienced death. To combat her depression, a psychodrama of her husband's death was enacted, with the wife as a participant. Someone assumed the husband's role and acted out the coronary attack. After the doctor pronounced the husband's death, the funeral and burial scenes were performed. Moreno offers the following description of the persuasive impact of this event on the bereaved wife:

You may say: "But Jack [the husband] is dead anyhow." Of course he is, but acting out the death scene brought back the dignity of the memory of the one she loved most in her life. The psychodrama brought her back to realizing herself and feeling herself as a wife of this man who she loved so much. It brought back the meaning of death and the meaning of our social etiquette of mourning for a man, of having a funeral—all things we modern people seem to ridicule. But many things which we think are ridiculous in reality have profound bearing on our feelings for those who have passed away (p. 282).

Here we see role playing used as a persuasive technique to alter the wife's attitudes about herself. To be sure, the scenario is linked to an external happening, the husband's death. But the woman's attitudes toward this event are not of primary import to the persuader; instead, his concern centers on ways that her attitudes toward the external event may affect her subsequent self-attitudes. By having reenacted the singular tragedy of the husband's death, the widow should be better equipped to cope with her potentially destructive self-attitudes of alienation and guilt.

Other examples of the persuasive efficacy of psychodramatic role playing can be offered. Drews (Moreno, 1957) described a case involving a woman who had married a man many years her senior. The couple wanted children, but the husband suffered from infertility. To solve the problem, both mates agreed to artificial insemination; a parental source was chosen, and the wife gave birth to a healthy baby boy.

Two years after the child's birth, the couple were divorced. Subsequently, the wife became severely depressed and attempted suicide. At the time she entered into a therapeutic relationship with Drews, the woman had rebounded from this psychological nadir; however, she still seemed to be experiencing considerable conflict. Analysis revealed that her conflict hinged on feelings of social ostracism, shame, and guilt—feelings occasioned by her perception that she had mothered an "artificial child." At a psychodramatic session she was afforded the opportunity to act out her feelings and attitudes about her maternal relationship with the son. Apparently, the experience eliminated her shame about the baby's conception. Drews gave this summary of the results:

This patient experienced a therapeutic catharsis through mind-body-action that could not be duplicated with any other therapeutic device known to psychiatry. She not only recovered from her recurrent anxiety but also rediscovered her self-esteem and became conscious of a deep and positive understanding of mothers in general and rejected children in particular (Moreno, pp. 284–285).

Thus, to the extent that Drews's conclusion are accurate, role playing served a dual persuasive function: it not only led to improvement in the mother's self-concept, it also influenced her perceptions of an important external social problem.

Obviously, the evidence in these two psychodramatic cases is anecdotal; neither instance provides a systematic test of the persuasive efficacy of role playing in modifying undesirable self-attitudes. Still, when viewed in conjunction with the more rigorous experimental research described earlier in this chapter, Moreno and Drews's accounts of the persuasive impact of psychodrama appear to be reasonable. The technique offers promise in dealing with unfavorable persuadee self-attitudes, and future researchers should aim at ascertaining the extent to which its promise can be realized.

Role playing is also an integral aspect of another recent approach to self-concept development and personal growth, the encounter group. Although not always therapeutic in the strictest sense, encounter groups seek heightened individual awareness of self-attitudes, as well as understanding of ways these self-attitudes affect the responses of others to the individual. In the typical encounter group, the trainer, or group leader, may often emerge as a principal persuasive force, even though all group members may alternately assume the roles of persuader and persuadee. The end products sought are more favorable participant self-attitudes and more functional, productive ways of dealing with the external environment. Moreover, incongruities between professed attitudes and actual behaviors are often exposed; "in group psychotherapy, with the help of group members, the therapist can see that while his clients say they wish to relate intimately with one another, their behavior says the opposite: that is the one thing they do not intend to do— reveal their hidden selves" (Forer, 1969, p. 34).

An interesting example of the cathartic effects of group role playing (here, of course, we assume that the catharsis should persuasively influence individual self-attitudes) is provided by Polster (1969). Members of a large encounter group were asked to role play scenes involving conversations between a hippie and a policeman. According to Polster's account, all members achieved a deep emotional involvement in the activity, which in turn led to a fuller understanding of themselves and their meanings for the situation:

The community involvement gave a cathartic and poetic line to the expression of 125 people. . . . The group discussed the meaning of the experience and the prevailing view was that people were expressing their suppressed aggression against the police—acting out in the role-playing situation what they would like to do in real life but have felt powerless (pp. 154–155).

Again, we see the close linkage that is likely to exist between perceptions of the external world and attitudes toward the self. Undoubtedly, suppressed aggression and resentment toward an external authority figure, the policeman, had a powerful influence on participants' self-perceptions. From a persuasive vantage point, the opportunity to act out their aggression under socially acceptable conditions probably resulted in a set of self-attitudes more harmonious with prevailing social circumstances.

More might be said about the use of role playing as a persuasive technique for altering self-attitudes, but we feel that the preceding remarks have captured the essential ingredients of the process. Perhaps in the past a disproportionate amount of research energy has been expended on the study of variables influencing persuadee response to messages dealing with issues and problems centered in the external world. In terms of the dichotomy we have employed herein, persuasion researchers have been more concerned with ways that an individual's self-attitudes affect his responses to the external world (e.g., his buying behaviors, his voting behaviors) than they have been with ways that the individual's attitudes and behaviors *vis-à-vis* the external world influence his perceptions of himself. The former line of research is by no means inconsequential, however, the time for a change of emphasis is at hand. In a world abounding in alienation, guilt, and self-doubt, we need to seek persuasive tools that will foster conditions conducive to personal growth and self-actualization. We have tried to demonstrate that role playing may be such a persuasive tool. Although the final verdict is not in, the possibility merits considerable scientific scrutiny.

---

an analysis of the persuasive dimensions of role playing

In this chapter, we have alluded several times to the difficulties attendant in specifying why role playing is an effective persuasive technique. Although we do not pretend to have a satisfactory answer to this question, we wish to conclude our discussion by specifying some of the features of role playing that may contribute to its persuasive impact.

IMMEDIACY

In a role-playing situation, the persuadee is thrust into an environment that closely simulates a threatening, anxiety-producing, real-life experience. If the cliché "Experience is the best teacher" has any validity, a dozen fatherly lectures about the possible harmful consequences of using drugs cannot substitute for the threat of one police arrest for a narcotics violation. One obvious limitation of living room lectures is their lack of immediacy; the intended persuadee can always deny that he would ever fall victim to such consequences. But when the consequences themselves are simulated, as in a role-playing situation, they loom as very real possibilities to the persuadee, possibilities that may facilitate attitude and behavior change.

Many institutions in our society have long recognized this fact. All the classroom lectures dealing with the wisdom of staying low when in a field of fire lack the persuasive impact of one journey through the infiltration course. The importance of proper driving attitudes is underscored more vividly by the simulator or the driving range than by any driver training text. Prospective doctors acquire functionally useful attitudes toward patients through simulated doctor–patient interactions. In each of the cases just mentioned, the immediacy of the situation enhances its persuasive potential. Perhaps, indeed, all the world's a stage, and perhaps our attitudes are most radically influenced when we are center stage.

PERSUADEE INVOLVEMENT

A consideration closely related to the immediacy of role-playing situations is that of persuadee involvement. We have already commented on the relatively passive stance assumed by the persuadee in the typical persuasive paradigm. Such passivity is foreign to the role-playing arena. As we observed earlier, the supposed lung cancer patient must articulate his fears and anxieties to the doctor. The grieving wife must participate in the reenactment of her husband's death. The hippie must release his pent-up frustrations to the police officer. If Bem (1965, 1968) is correct in asserting that an individual's attitudes are often inferred from his behaviors, it follows that role-playing behavior should trigger cognitive processes that result in attitude change.

The importance of involvement in the role-playing experience is underscored by the previously discussed findings of Mann (1967). Recall that among male subjects, high verbalizers (i.e., persons highly involved in the role play) reported more attitude change than did low verbalizers. It is tempting to liken these low verbalizers to the persuadee of the typical persuasive paradigm. While they are bombarded by numerous appeals of the persuader, they remain psychologically aloof from the situation, and this aloofness confers a large measure of persuasive immunity. By contrast, high verbalizers are psychologically attuned to the situation; in the current idiom, they are into the ongoing interaction, which seeks to alter existing attitudes and behaviors.

NONVERBAL MESSAGE ELEMENTS

When compared with the traditional persuasive paradigm, role-playing situations place greater emphasis on the nonverbal dimensions of a persuasive transaction. Consider, for instance, the single act of the doctor pointing to the supposed cancer patient's chest X-ray, a role-playing behavior used in the study of Janis and Mann. The impact of this simple behavioral sequence may well transcend the effects of an extended medical lecture on the dangers of cigarette smoking. Likewise, the many facial nuances of the doctor add to the drama of the exchange. An experienced persuader may be able to manipulate certain nonverbal message elements in the traditional persuasive setting, but it is doubtful that the effect is as marked as it is in the role-playing situation.

Numerous students of persuasion have testified to the importance of the nonverbal band; in fact, some have argued that more persuasion takes place through nonverbal than through verbal means. If this is the case, the heightened importance of nonverbal communication in role-playing situations may help to explain the persuasive efficacy of the technique.

summing up

In this chapter we have considered the use of role playing as a persuasive strategy. Although research dealing with the persuasive efficacy of role-playing experiences is not extensive, such experiences appear to have the potential for changing both attitudes toward a controversial issue and attitudes toward the self.

Regardless of whether we have isolated the factors contributing most heavily to the persuasive impact of the role-playing experience, we believe we have demonstrated its potential importance as a new technique of persuasion. Given the contemporary societal value for involvement, we expect researcher and practitioner alike to devote increasingly more attention to role playing. Although the technique is not likely to replace traditional approaches to persuasion, role playing is certain to augment them, with the end result of providing the potential persuader with a broader repertory of persuasive strategies.

COUNTERATTITUDINAL ADVOCACY AS A PERSUASIVE TECHNIQUE: THEORETICAL INTERPRETATIONS

Earlier in this volume we described the essential elements of a persuasive paradigm which we labeled *counterattitudinal advocacy* (Figure 4, p. 00). While granting that counterattitudinal advocacy is a form of role playing, we hold that it differs from the generalized case of role playing in at least two ways. First, the situational factors associated with counterattitudinal advocacy are somewhat more easily specified; second, the communication transaction, at least in terms of message preparation and presentation, is somewhat more structured in cases involving counterattitudinal advocacy.

Recall that the use of counterattitudinal advocacy as a persuasive strategy requires that the intended persuadee be induced to publicly encode a message demonstrably at odds with his prior beliefs. Given certain minimal circumstances, the persuader assumes that the persuadee's belief-discrepant communication behavior will trigger a change in his attitudes or behaviors, that he will become more favorably disposed toward the position advocated in the message. Thus, in the example used in Chapter 1, the father (persuader) attempted to engender less favorable attitudes toward pot smoking on the part of his son (persuadee) by inducing the son to prepare and present an anti-marijuana message for some real or ostensible target audience.

The persuasive efficacy of counterattitudinal advocacy is well documented in the research literature. In fact, so much attention has been directed to this particular new technique of persuasion that we devote two chapters to it. In this chapter, we consider some of the theoretical interpretations or explanations of counterattitudinal advocacy effects; in Chapter 5, we examine research dealing with some of the variables that may heighten or reduce the persuasive impact of counterattitudinal advocacy. An understanding of these theories and variables should make both persuader and persuadee more sensitive to the potential uses of counterattitudinal advocacy as a persuasive technique.

the "early" dissonance interpretation of counterattitudinal advocacy effects

Festinger (1957) was one of the first writers to offer a comprehensive theory capable of accounting for the persuasive impact of counterattitudinal advocacy. His theory of cognitive dissonance, like other cognitive consistency theories (e.g., Newcomb, 1953; Heider, 1958; Osgood & Tannenbaum, 1955; Rokeach & Rothman, 1965), assumes that persons strive to maintain consistency among all their cognitions or ideas, an assumption discussed briefly in Chapter 2. When an inconsistent cognition enters the system, the individual experiences an unpleasant psychological state called *cognitive dissonance*. Moreover, because of the unpleasant characteristics of dissonance, the person is motivated to behave in some way calculated to restore *cognitive consonance*.

How can the basic postulates of cognitive dissonance theory be applied to situations involving counterattitudinal advocacy? Festinger and Carlsmith (1959) argue that in such situations dissonance is created by the conflicting cognitions: 1 / I believe x, and 2 / I am advocating (or am irrevocably committed to advocating) *not-x*. In other words, people in our society are taught that it is at least foolish and at most immoral to publicly advocate things in which they do not believe. Consequently, when they become ensnared in such a communicative trap, they experience cognitive dissonance.

Since dissonance is uncomfortable, the counterattitudinal advocate will behave in some way calculated to reduce it. One possible means of reducing dissonance is to change attitudes or behavior; that is, the advocate may alter the cognition "I believe x" so that it becomes "I believe *not-x*." When such a cognitive change occurs, private belief becomes consistent with public behavior. And when viewed as a persuasive strategy, such a change signals successful influence, for the intended persuadee has, in a sense, persuaded himself to accept the position championed by the persuader. If our hypothetical son experiences dissonance because of inconsistency between his public anti-marijuana statements and his private pro-marijuana attitudes, and if he reduces his dissonance by adopting less favorable attitudes toward marijuana, the father's influence attempt has succeeded.

Certain implications of this "early" dissonance interpretation merit discussion. Unlike several other theoretical explanations of counterattitudinal advocacy effects, the "early" dissonance position does not necessarily require the persuadee to prepare and to present a message. For as long as the persuadee perceives that he is irrevocably committed to the task—that he has agreed to encode a belief-discrepant message and that there is no way for him to back out—he should experience dissonance resulting from inconsistency between private belief and public assent. A skillful persuader thus has only to secure the persuadee's commitment to behave counterattitudinally in order to activate the processes of attitude and behavior change; "early" dissonance theorizing suggests that our hypothetical son's commitment to encode an anti-marijuana message may be sufficient to alter his attitudes toward pot and his subsequent decisions about smoking it.

A key problem in the dissonance formulation is embodied in the phrase "behave *in some way* calculated to reduce dissonance." This phrase acknowledges that attitude or behavior change consistent with the message position is only one of numerous dissonance-reducing avenues open to the counterattitudinal advocate. Naturally, when counterattitudinal advocacy involves persuasive intent, the persuader hopes that the persuadee will choose the attitude change mode. But if certain circumstances prevail, the persuadee may reduce dissonance in other ways. These circumstances are discussed in detail in Chapter 5; however, mention of several of them at this point should further clarify the "early" dissonance interpretation.

Suppose an individual is offered considerable justification for adopting a counterattitudinal position. For instance, in our customary example, the father may seek to induce the son to encode an anti-marijuana message by offering him a large sum of money. If this happened, the son could reason as follows: even though I am saying something I do not believe, I am being rewarded handsomely for saying it. Consequently, my behavior is perfectly justified; for this much payment, I'll be happy to say things I don't believe any time.

In other words, high justification has one or both of the following effects: it reduces the dissonance a counterattitudinal advocate experiences, or it provides a readily invoked mode of dissonance reduction. Thus it becomes unnecessary to change attitudes or behavior; if the son is paid a large sum of money for denouncing marijuana, he would not be expected to change his attitudes and behaviors in respect to it. Specifically, the "early" dissonance interpretation of counterattitudinal advocacy effects holds that justification is negatively related to dissonance and subsequent attitude or behavior change: *the less the justification for counterattitudinal advocacy, the greater the magnitude of dissonance and subsequent attitude or behavior change.* Therefore, if the persuader wishes to maximize the likelihood of persuasive success, he must induce the persuadee to encode the belief-discrepant message for as little justification as possible.

Choice is another important variable in the "early" dissonance formulation. If a person feels that he has little or no choice about engaging in counterattitudinal advocacy, he should not experience much dissonance. Conversely, if perceived choice is high, dissonance should be magnified, since the advocate is not only faced with the uncomfortable cognition that he is encoding counterattitudinally; but in addition, he perceives that he could have chosen to do otherwise. In a sense, lack of perceived choice is the negative side of the justification coin, for the lament, "What else could I have done!" justifies the dissonance-producing activity of encoding a belief-discrepant message. Should the father threaten to cut off the son's allowance for six months if he fails to prepare an anti-marijuana message, the son will probably comply; however, it is unlikely he will alter his attitudes or behaviors regarding pot smoking.

Finally, effort is a factor that influences the persuasive impact of counterattitudinal advocacy. The "early" dissonance position posits that effort and self-persuasion are directly related: *the more effort expended in counterattitudinal advocacy, the greater the dissonance and subsequent self-persuasion.* When considerable effort accompanies belief-discrepant encoding, the advocate experiences an additional dissonance-producing cognition; not only is he publicly supporting a position he does not espouse, he is also working hard to advance it. Conversely, if energy expenditure is low, the advocate may rationalize away his behavior by reasoning that it has not required much commitment on his part.

In a nutshell: the "early" dissonance interpretation attributes the persuasive efficacy of counterattitudinal advocacy to cognitive inconsistency between private belief and public behavior. For a persuader to employ counterattitudinal advocacy effectively, he must induce the persuadee to encode, or irrevocably commit himself to encode, a belief-discrepant message. Additionally, however, the persuader must concern himself with other factors associated with the situation. He must seek to provide barely enough justification to induce the persuadee to comply with his request. He must strive to structure the environment so as to provide the persuadee with a high level of perceived choice. And finally, the task must be demanding enough to ensure a fair amount of energy expenditure by the persuadee. If these conditions are met, "early" dissonance theory suggests that the act of counterattitudinal advocacy will have a powerful impact on the persuadee's attitudes and behaviors, and that the persuadee will persuade himself to adopt the initially belief-discrepant position he has publicly advocated.

the "later" dissonance interpretation of counterattitudinal advocacy effects

How often does the average person engage in a debate or take the role of devil's advocate? Who has never told a "white lie" to spare the feelings of an acquaintance? Activities of this kind have recently caused some writers to question the efficacy of the "early" dissonance interpretation of counterattitudinal advocacy effects. We have all debated, played devil's advocate, or told white lies, but it is doubtful that these communicative acts have caused us to modify our attitudes or behaviors toward the issues in question. A garish, unattractive dress is still garish and unattractive, no matter how enthusiastically we assure a friend that we admire her sartorial discernment.

One may ask why little self-persuasion occurs in these situations, even though public behavior is obviously at odds with private beliefs. Apparently, it is because the rules of the situation allow us to lie with cognitive impunity. Even though some educators disapprove of the practice, participants in most scholastic debates are allowed to argue either side of the issue. Dormitory bull sessions are enlivened and made more stimulating by the presence of a devil's advocate. And in the case of the white lie, counterattitudinal advocacy serves a socially desirable end; namely, it spares the feelings of a friend or acquaintance over a matter of trivial import. Only the most socially insensitive persons respond to a request for reinforcement by stating, "That's the most hideous dress I've ever seen!"

Perhaps, then, dissonance does not result from mere inconsistency between public and private assent, but rather from other features associated with counterattitudinal advocacy. Specifically, recent theorizing holds that dissonance is present or absent to the extent the advocate perceives that aversive consequences will result from his counterattitudinal act. Aronson (1968) puts the matter this way:

In the experiments on counterattitudinal advocacy, for example, I would suggest that it is incorrect to say that dissonance existed between the cognitions "I believe the task is dull" [private belief] and "I told someone that the task was interesting" [public behavior]. . . . What is dissonant is the cognition "I am a decent, truthful human being" and the cognition "I have misled a person; I have conned him into believing something which just isn't true; he thinks that I really believe it and I cannot set him straight because I probably won't see him again" (p. 24).

In the same vein, Carlsmith (1968) asserts that "any time a person makes some statement counter to his attitudes, and a listener (whose opinion is important to the speaker) is unaware of both the speaker's attitudes and his motivations for speaking against these attitudes, dissonance will be aroused" (p. 806).

To drive home the distinction between "early" and "later" dissonance interpretations, contrast the following situations: our hypothetical son telling a white lie about a friend's new suit as opposed to the same youth presenting anti-marijuana arguments to a group of peers known to be generally uncommitted on the issue of pot smoking. In the first instance, the son's behavior will have no aversive social consequences; on the contrary, he has behaved in a socially desirable way toward his friend. Consequently, even though public behavior is inconsistent with private belief, little dissonance and subsequent self-persuasion would be expected.

In the second case, however, the son's act is laden with potential aversive consequences. For to the extent that he actually subscribes to the proposition that pot smoking is a good thing, he perceives that he may be conning his uncommitted peers into assuming an anti-marijuana stance, a circumstance not in their best interests. Moreover, his behavior may also produce undesirable outcomes for himself, for there is the possibility that one of his acquaintances who knows his actual feelings about pot may discover what he has done. Such a discovery reflects unfavorably on the son; it casts him in the role of a liar and a hypocrite. Given this array of potential aversive consequences, the son should experience considerable dissonance, which may be resolved by adopting more negative attitudes toward the use of marijuana.

The preceding example focuses on two possible

sources of aversive consequences associated with counterattitudinal advocacy. The first of these concerns harmful outcomes for the advocate's real or ostensible target audience. If a counterattitudinal message is unlikely to cause an audience to adopt harmful beliefs or behaviors, its effects are psychologically benign; if the acceptance of harmful beliefs or behaviors seems probable, its impact is psychologically malignant. This suggests that, in terms of "later" dissonance theorizing, an initially uncommitted audience provides the greatest potential for dissonance arousal. For if the audience members are initially firmly opposed or firmly in favor of the position taken in the belief-discrepant message, the advocate may derive solace from their apparent intractability. If, on the other hand, the members lack a strong initial attitude about the issue, they are easy persuasive prey for the advocate, a circumstance calculated to generate considerable dissonance. In Chapter 5, we examine studies dealing with the influence of initial audience attitude on the self-persuasion process.

A second source of aversive consequences is found in possible harmful outcomes for the counterattitudinal advocate himself. As a result of lying to an impressionable audience, the advocate's self-image may suffer, particularly if he believes that his duplicity will be discovered. Obviously, such considerations are differentially important to people. A person with low self-esteem may feel he has behaved consistently by selling out his own private convictions, whereas an individual with high self-esteem is likely to be intensely perturbed by such actions. Naturally, the latter should experience more dissonance—and hence be more susceptible to self-persuasion—than the former.

By the same token, people who see nothing morally reprehensible about manipulating others should be less concerned about others' perceptions of their behaviors; in fact, as we have argued elsewhere (Burgoon, Miller, & Tubbs, 1972), such persons may find it intrinsically rewarding to be placed in a situation with a high potential for successful influence. Thus, Machavellian types of counterattitudinal advocates with a high need to influence should have greater immunity to dissonance resulting from perceived aversive consequences for themselves—or, for that matter, for the target audience as well.

Two points about the "later" dissonance interpretation should be considered. First, advocates of this position have not deserted cognitive dissonance as an explanation of counterattitudinal advocacy effects; instead, they have redefined the source of dissonance arousal. As a result, the role of variables such as justification, effort, and choice remains relatively constant for both the "early" and "late" dissonance interpretations. One significant departure in viewpoint concerns the initial attitudes of the real or ostensible target audience: whereas "early" dissonance theorizing suggests that initial attitude is an irrelevant variable, "later" dissonance formulations hold that an initially uncommitted audience generates more dissonance, and eventually more self-persuasion. This disagreement constitutes the major empirical difference between the two viewpoints.

Second, readers with an applied persuasive bent may feel that the differences just discussed are little more than a scholarly tempest in a teapot, that they are of limited import for the use of counterattitudinal advocacy as a practical persuasive strategy. In a theoretical sense, we concur with this judgment. As Miller has argued (in Mortensen & Sereno [eds.], *Advances in Communication Research*, 1972):

The issue appears to involve a rather subtle distinction not easily probed by present methodological tools. For the Festinger position ["early" dissonance] can be maintained by arguing that in the above situations [situations involving debates and white lies] *some* dissonance is aroused, but that the accompanying consonant cognitions assure its resolution with little or no change in overt behavior. For example, consider the white lie; suppose I tell a friend that a hideous tie is quite becoming. Aronson holds that this statement will not produce dissonance. However, perhaps some dissonance is produced but quickly dissipated by the consonant cognitions "I am saying something pleasing to a friend" and "The whole thing is trivial, anyway." In fact, introspection tells me I sometimes do experience tension under such circumstances, especially if the tie is *exceedingly* hideous.

Still, although the distinction remains a theoretical enigma, we would suggest it has practical implications for the potential persuader. As we have noted, a person's choice of the "early" or "later" dissonance interpretation dictates his decision about the importance of the initial audience attitude variable. If he is an advocate of "early" dissonance theorizing, the persuader assumes that the attitudinal makeup of the ostensible target audience is irrelevant; he has only to induce the persuadee to encode counterattitudinally for a real or ostensible set of receivers. Conversely, if the persuader embraces the "later" dissonance interpretation, audience makeup is of crucial import, for the persuadee should be led to believe that his receivers are initially uncommitted on the counterattitudinal issue.

Moreover, "early" dissonance theory seems to imply that all persons are equally susceptible to dissonance (although perhaps this is an oversimplification). By emphasizing the moral and personal dimensions of dissonance arousal, "later" dissonance implies that such is not the case. Some people are certain to be more concerned than others about the ethical consequences of lying. Some people evince more concern than others about self-concept. People differ about the kinds of events that are damaging to self-concept; one man's disaster may be another's triumph. All these factors suggest that the persuader should undertake careful individual analysis of the intended persuadee. For only if these individual differences are well understood is it possible to structure a counterattitudinal advocacy situation calculated to result in maximum persuasive impact.

the incentive interpretation of counterattitudinal advocacy effects

Thus far, while considering the two dissonance interpretations of counterattitudinal advocacy effects, we have emphasized the negative since both "early" and "later" dissonance theorizing hold that self-persuasion follows the arousal of cognitive dissonance, which is an unpleasant drive state. In sharp contrast, incentive theory (Janis & Gilmore, 1965; Janis, 1968), in the words of an old song, accentuates the positive aspects surrounding counterattitudinal advocacy. For these theorists, magnitude of self-persuasion following counterattitudinal advocacy is directly related to the positive rewards, or incentives, associated with counterattitudinal advocacy. In an early articulation of the position, Janis and Gilmore assert:

When a person accepts the task of improvising arguments in favor of a point of view at variance with his own personal convictions, he becomes temporarily motivated to think up all the good positive arguments he can, and at the same time, suppresses thoughts about the negative arguments which are supposedly irrelevant to the assigned task. This "biased scanning" increases the salience of the positive arguments and therefore increases the chances of acceptance of the new attitude position. *A gain in attitude change would not be expected, however, if resentment or other interfering affective reactions were aroused by negative incentives in the role-playing situation* (pp. 17–18) [italics ours].

A later statement by Janis further underscores the need for positive incentives by positing two necessary conditions if attitude change is to follow counterattitudinal advocacy. First, the counterattitudinal advocate must recall or invent arguments that will serve as positive incentives for accepting a new attitude position; second, the advocate's psychological set must foster open-minded exploration of the arguments' positive incentive values, rather than a negative reaction of hostility or suspicion.

To illustrate the application of incentive theory, return again to our hypothetical father and son. Assume that the son has agreed to prepare and present an anti-marijuana message, a task at odds with his beliefs. To accomplish this end, the son is forced to think about arguments against the use of marijuana. This, itself, may be no small demand, since he may have had few occasions to consider arguments opposing pot smoking. But to the extent that he is successful in his "biased scanning" (i.e., his attempts to call up good belief-discrepant arguments and to suppress relevant belief-congruent ones), he will be able to construct a persuasive counterattitudinal message.

Incentive theory posits that his success hinges on the presence of positive rewards or incentives which are linked to the encoding process. These incentives may take the form of monetary payment, attractive characteristics of the person sponsoring the request for counterattitudinal advocacy (in a case involving persuasive intent, this is often the persuader himself), or another "good" reason for engaging in the counterattitudinal task. Thus, if the son regards his father as an attractive sponsor or if the father offers the son reasonable payment for preparing an anti-marijuana message, the likelihood of self-persuasion is enhanced.

The preceding discussion emphasizes several important differences between incentive and dissonance theory interpretations of counterattitudinal advocacy effects. Unlike dissonance theory, the incentive position holds that attitude or behavior change requires covert or overt message encoding. Since change results from biased scanning of previously belief-discrepant arguments, mere commitment to engage in counterattitudinal advocacy is insufficient for activating attitude change processes. If our hypothetical son is to adopt more negative attitudes toward pot smoking, he must weigh and consider anti-marijuana arguments, not just agree to encode a counterattitudinal message.

Most important, incentive theorizing posits a direct relation between justification and subsequent self-persuasion: *the greater the justification, the greater the resultant self-persuasion.* Unlike dissonance theory, which contends a man should be paid a bare minimum for lying, incentive theory argues that he should be rewarded handsomely. At first glance, then, the two interpretations appear to generate clearly contradictory predictions about the role of justification in counterattitudinal advocacy. Moreover, the two conflicting views may seem to lend themselves to unequivocal experimental ajudication. As we demonstrate in Chapter 5, the issue is not this simple; in fact, present research evidence suggests the two theories are complementary, rather than antagonistic.

Aside from justification, the two formulations apparently agree on the effects of other variables discussed previously, though, of course, for different reasons. Incentive theory views low perceived choice as a negative incentive likely to engender feelings of resentment and hostility; consequently, as with dissonance theory, the relative absence of choice should inhibit the persuasive impact of counterattitudinal advocacy. Effort is an essential ingredient of the biased scanning process; indeed, the basic postulate of incentive theory states that positive incentives will increase the energy expended in biased scanning, thereby culminating in greater self-persuasion. Thus justification is the only variable that engenders disagreement between dissonance and incentive theorists. This disagreement seems to pose a dilemma for the persuasion practitioner seeking to implement the technique of counterattitudinal advocacy: should he offer the intended persuadee considerable justification for belief-discrepant encoding, or should he attempt to keep justification at a bare minimum? Before despairing, however, the research evidence discussed in the next chapter should be carefully weighed, since it provides at least a partial reconciliation of the two interpretations and suggests that other variables may determine whether a strategy of high or low justification should be employed.

---

the self–perception interpretation of counterattitudinal advocacy effects

Probably no contemporary behavioral scientist has been as influential as B. F. Skinner. Therefore, it is hardly surprising that one current theorist (Bem, 1965, 1968) has invoked Skinnerian concepts to explain the persuasive efficacy of counterattitudinal advocacy.

The key to Bem's self-perception interpretation, mentioned briefly in Chapter 3, is contained in the following assumption: *people often make inferences about their attitudes by observing their own behaviors*. This deceptively simple statement departs radically from most persuasion literature, which treats behavior as a consequence of attitudes, rather than as a precursor of them. To illustrate the distinction, we can turn again to our hypothetical son. Traditionally, the student of persuasion might assume that the son's positive attitude toward marijuana causes him to engage in pot smoking behavior. Bem argues that from the son's perspective the sequence can be reversed; he may infer he has a positive attitude about marijuana by observing the fact that he is always smoking it. In making this inference, the son has used the same datum others would employ when judging his attitudes about the use of marijuana. Thus, if his father were asked if the son has a favorable attitude toward marijuana, he might answer, "I guess he does; he's always smoking it."

Of course, not all behaviors provide an unambiguous basis for drawing inferences about underlying attitudes. Suppose the son is strongly attracted to a particular group of student peers, that these students constitute a reference group with whom he wishes to affiliate. Moreover, assume that occasional use of marijuana is a norm of the group. One evening the group decides to smoke together, and the son is invited to join them in the activity. He complies, hoping that this action will assure his acceptance by the other group members.

In this instance, the son is not likely to infer positive attitudes about marijuana from his pot smoking activities. For in smoking marijuana with the group, he is engaged in manding behavior (i.e., his smoking responses are under the control of a specific reinforcer, the possibility of acceptance by a highly desirable reference group). Since he is aware of this fact, he will be unwilling to assess his attitudes by observing his behavior.

The preceding discussion suggests that if certain external circumstances exist, the individual, as well as others, uses his behavior as a basis for inferring his attitudes. Conversely, given differing circumstances, all parties will hesitate to make the same inference. Bem puts the matter this way:

Individuals come to "know" their own attitudes and other internal states partially by inferring them from observations of their own overt behavior and the circumstances in which it occurs. Thus, to the extent that information from external cues is weak, ambiguous, or uninterpretable, the individual is functioning in the same position as an outside observer of this behavior, an observer who, necessarily, must rely on those same external cues to infer the individual's inner states (Bem & McConnell, 1970, p. 23).

How does self-perception theory apply to the interpretation of counterattitudinal advocacy effects? Consider two situations, one in which a person is offered considerable justification for engaging in counterattitudinal advocacy and a second in which justification is barely minimal. In the first instance, the advocate, like our hypothetical son, is likely to perceive that he is manding reinforcement from the environment; consequently, he will be reluctant to infer that his behavior gives him valid information about his underlying attitudes. But in the second situation, the likelihood of inferring attitudes from behavior is greater, for the external grounds for making the statements are negligible. Thus, when induced to engage in counterattitudinal advocacy, "low-compensation [advocates] infer that they must agree with the arguments . . . whereas high—compensation [advocates] discard their behavior as a relevant guide to their 'actual' attitudes" (Bem & McConnell, 1970, p. 24).

Like dissonance theory, then, the self-perception formulation posits an inverse relation between justification and self-persuasion. Moreover, the hypothesized effects of choice and effort are identical for the two theories. Bem and the dissonance theorists do not disagree on what will happen in counterattitudinal advocacy situations, but rather on the reasons for what occurs. For the dissonance theorist, low justification heightens the dissonance experienced by the counterattitudinal advocate; for Bem, low justification creates an external environment that causes the advocate to infer that his behaviors are indicative of his underlying attitudes. In both cases, low justification enhances the persuasive efficacy of counterattitudinal advocacy.

If dissonance and self-perception have identical implications for the persuasion practitioner, why concern ourselves with a discussion of both theories? Our motive is not to endorse one approach as more tenable than the other, for as we show in Chapter 5, it is difficult if not impossible to conduct a crucial test of the two theories. Perhaps, in the final analysis, our decision stems from the conviction that those who employ counterattitudinal advocacy as a persuasive technique should know as much as possible about it. And this knowledge should not be limited to the behavioral effects of counterattitudinal advocacy, it should extend to the various internal processes that conceivably account for these behavioral outcomes. Dissonance and self-perception represent two distinct sets of internal processes used to explain the same behavioral consequences. Which, if either, is correct? Only time and further research can shed light on this question.

summing up

In this chapter we have examined four theoretical interpretations of counterattitudinal advocacy effects. Our discussion has by no means exhausted the possibilities. Baron (1968) and Kelman et al. (1969) have formulated a functional analysis interpretation of counterattitudinal advocacy effects, an interpretation yielding predictions somewhat at variance with other theories. Likewise, Kelley's (1967) attribution theory, although dealing with a wider range of behavioral events, can be applied to situations involving counterattitudinal advocacy. Finally, Berger (1971) has recently begun work on a theory that seeks to apply the constructs of role theory—particularly, role competence—to the counterattitudinal advocacy arena. We have not discussed these positions in detail, however, they may well provide valuable future leads for persuasion researcher and practitioner alike.

For the practitioner, the importance of these theories lies in the implications they carry for the development of persuasive strategy. For the researcher, their value is determined by the extent to which they provide tenable explanations of the persuasive effects of counterattitudinal advocacy. In both instances, the acid test of each theory is provided by assessing the extent of its explanatory harmony with research findings. In the next chapter, we examine some of the findings.

COUNTERATTITUDINAL ADVOCACY AS A PERSUASIVE TECHNIQUE: RESEARCH FINDINGS

There exists a voluminous research literature dealing with the problem of counterattitudinal advocacy, but it is well beyond the scope of this volume to attempt an exhaustive summary of this work. Consequently, we have selected some studies that bear directly on the theoretical issues posed in Chapter 4. Moreover, in keeping with our major purpose, we have attempted to underscore the implications of these studies for the persuasion practitioner. It is impossible to tie together all existing loose ends, but a careful reading of this chapter should provide both persuader and persuadee with a better grasp of the variables influencing the persuasive impact of counterattitudinal advocacy.

justification

As might be expected from considering the various theoretical interpretations, the lion's share of research has been devoted to investigating the role of justification in counterattitudinal advocacy. Since justification can be operationally defined in numerous ways, we consider two types of justification: justification based on amount of monetary payment and justification based on the type of sponsorship associated with the counterattitudinal encoding request. Although these are not the only ways that the variable has been manipulated, they capture the flavor of the research thus far conducted.

JUSTIFICATION BASED ON AMOUNT OF MONETARY PAYMENT

An appropriate starting point for examining the effects of monetary justification on self-persuasion is the classic study of Festinger and Carlsmith (1959). Not surprisingly, they hypothesized an inverse relationship between monetary justification and subsequent self-persuasion, a hypothesis based on the "early" dissonance formulation. In order to establish a general model for the research that follows, we describe their study in some detail.

Subjects were first asked to perform a dull, monotonous task. After engaging in the task for a time, they were instructed to rate its attractiveness. Consistent with expectations, all subjects perceived the task as dull and banal.

Next the fun began. Each subject was told by the experimenter that an assistant normally was stationed in the outer office to greet the next arrival and to tell him the enjoyable, interesting aspects of the task. Unfortunately, the assistant had been unavoidably detained. Would the subject be willing to aid the experimenter by assuming this role for about an hour and by "being on call" for possible future assistance? If so, he would be paid for his trouble. Half the subjects, randomly assigned to the high-justification treatment, were then quoted a salary of $20; the other half, randomly assigned to the low-justification treatment, were offered $1. Almost all the subjects complied with the experimenter's request.

Consider what has just been described from the perspective of an influence attempt. The persuader (experimenter) has induced the persuadees (subjects) to encode counterattitudinally (i.e., the persuadees have agreed to tell people that a dull, banal task is interesting and enjoyable). Moreover, the persuader has structured the situation so that the magnitude of monetary justification associated with counterattitudinal advocacy has been systematically varied: half the advocates will receive $20 and the other half will be paid only $1. For those still puzzled about how counterattitudinal advocacy can be used as a persuasive technique, Festinger and Carlsmith's manipulation provides a working example.

Shortly after each subject sat down in the outer office, the next "subject" (actually the real assistant of the experimenter) arrived. The arriving "subject" asked the supposed assistant how he had liked the experiment, and the latter replied the task had been quite enjoyable and interesting. The arriving "subject" took issue with this assertion, stating that several of his friends had reported that the experiment was boring. For the next 15 or 20 minutes a lively dialogue ensued, with the subject engaged in the counterattitudinal task of attempting to convince the actual assistant that the experiment would be interesting and enjoyable. The dialogue ended when the experimenter arrived, purportedly to escort the "subject" to the experiment.

The actual subject was then thanked for his help and told that he was free to leave. Before departing, however, he was asked to answer a few more questions about the original experiment. Among them was an item used to obtain a second rating of the experimental task. As indicated, Festinger and Carlsmith hypothesized that on this second rating, persons receiving $1 for engaging in counterattitudinal advocacy would increase their attractiveness ratings of the dull task significantly more than persons paid $20.

The results confirmed this hypothesis and are interpreted as supporting the "early" dissonance formulation. Persons receiving low monetary justification experience more dissonance, and in turn, dissonance is reduced by becoming more favorably disposed toward the dull task. On the other hand, those persons receiving high monetary justification should experience little dissonance, and if dissonance does occur, it can be readily reduced by emphasizing the handsome reward extended for engaging in counterattitudinal advocacy. Thus these persons do not need to reevaluate their attitudes toward the boring task.

On the face of it, then, the lesson learned from the Festinger and Carlsmith study seems to be unambiguous: if counterattitudinal advocacy is to be used as a persuasive strategy, the persuader should provide the persuadee with minimal justification for engaging in belief-discrepant encoding. Unfortunately, the matter is not that simple, for the study has attracted many critics. Most objections have centered on the manipulation of monetary justification. Whereas Festinger and Carlsmith assumed that $1 was a minimally sufficient payment and $20 an equitable salary, other writers have argued that $20 is an inordinately large payment for the task involved. If so, the payment would not engender perceptions of adequate justification; rather, it would create feelings of suspicion and hostility—negative incentives that would interfere with the job of open-minded counterattitudinal encoding. A later study by Rosenberg (1965) offered some support for this latter interpretation.

Dissonance theorists have countered these criticisms by pointing to subsequent work by Cohen (Brehm & Cohen, 1962). His study employed four levels of monetary justification: $0.50, $1, $5, and $10. Yale students were randomly assigned to each of the four conditions and were asked by the experimenter to write an essay favoring the position of the New Haven police following a recent riot on the campus which had resulted in charges of police brutality. The experimenter *assumed:* (1) that motivation and interest in this topic on the part of the subjects were high, (2) that all subjects were sympathetic toward the students and extremely negative toward the police and, therefore, (3) that writing a pro-police essay would constitute a counterattitudinal act for the subjects.

After writing the essay, all subjects completed an attitude measure designed to assess their feelings about the actions of the police. Consistent with the dissonance prediction, subjects paid $0.50 for engaging in counterattitudinal advocacy reported significantly more favorable attitudes toward the actions of the police than did subjects in any of the other three conditions. Obviously, say the dissonance theorists, one would not expect marked differences in suspicion between the $0.50 and $1 payments. Still, as expected, subjects receiving $0.50 report significantly more self-persuasion following counterattitudinal advocacy.

Bem (1965) has replicated Cohen's findings, using a somewhat different methodology. He argues, however, that the results should be interpreted from a self-perception, rather than a dissonance framework. Bem's view is that subjects in the $0.50 condition do not change their attitudes because of dissonance arousal; instead, given the minimal payment, they infer pro-police attitudes from their pro-police essay-writing behaviors.

Several problems seem to plague studies that seek to manipulate justification by varying monetary payment. First, few of the studies have attempted to assess the meanings that subjects assign to particular amounts of money; instead, the researcher has made the payment decisions on the basis of his meanings for the situation. In many cases, the perceptions of subject and researcher may differ radically. For example, Berger (1969) paid high-justification subjects $2.50 to encode counterattitudinally, whereas low-justification subjects received $0.50. After the task had been completed, all subjects were asked to rate the adequacy of the monetary payment. High-justification subjects reported a mean rating of 4.0 on a four-point scale; in other words, they all rated the payment as maximally adequate. By contrast, the mean rating for low-justification subjects was about 3.0. Although these two ratings differ significantly, a rating of 3.0 on a four-point scale certainly does not reflect a very low evaluation of adequacy of payment. Interestingly, when asked why they rated the $0.50 payment so high, several subjects said that they had never before been paid anything for participating in research. Given this comparative yardstick, it is not surprising they chose to rate the payment as adequate. And it should be emphasized that the Berger study is one of the few in which manipulation checks have been used to probe subject perceptions of monetary payment.

Manipulation problems may also result from the presence of numerous other justifying circumstances in the counterattitudinal advocacy situation. For instance, every scientific study is potentially justified because the subject is supposedly contributing to knowledge. To the extent that such a venture is valued, the subject may feel that a request for counterattitudinal encoding is justified, even if he is paid nothing for doing it. Moreover, mere participation in a study may require considerable effort. If a person travels a distance to participate in research, he will probably feel that his behavior is justified by the energy exerted to get there. In fact, several subjects in the Berger study reported they were willing to complete the counterattitudinal encoding task because they had walked a good distance on a rainy day to be in the study. Given all the potential sources of justification that may intrude on the counterattitudinal advocacy situation, it is not surprising that attempts to manipulate the single dimension of monetary justification often meet with limited success.

The preceding problems can best be illustrated by referring once again to our hypothetical father and son. Suppose the father, in his role as persuader, opts for the dissonance approach; that is, he decides to offer his son low monetary payment for preparing an anti-marijuana message. After some thought, he hits on a figure of $2, an amount he perceives as minimal. But how is he to know the son will also define $2 as a miserly sum? Perhaps for the latter, the acquisition of $2 represents a significant improvement in his financial condition. If so, the level of monetary justification, from the point of view of the intended persuadee, is high, rather than low.

Of course, the father may resolve this problem by asking the son to encode for nothing, by offering him no monetary payment whatsoever. If he chooses this alternative, how is he to assess other possible justifying circumstances that may be associated with the counterattitudinal request? Perhaps the son feels that he has little or no choice in the matter, that if he refuses to prepare the message, he will be the victim of intolerable punishment. As we noted earlier, such lack of perceived choice constitutes a negative dimension of the justification variable. Or the son may hold his father in high esteem; he may consider that the source of the counterattitudinal request provides sufficient justification for complying ("If my father wants me to do it, that's reason enough for me!"). In other words, positive sponsorship may provide the advocate with ample justification for engaging in counterattitudinal advocacy. We turn now to research that has examined this possibility.

One of the first attempts to manipulate justification in terms of sponsorship occurs in a study by Janis and Gilmore (1965). Operating from an incentive theory framework, they hypothesized that positive sponsorship would result in greater self-persuasion than would negative sponsorship. Specifically, Janis and Gilmore state:

Among the obvious instances of negative incentives would be information that lowers the prestige of the sponsor or that leads to him being perceived as a manipulative person who is trying to influence people for his own personal aggrandizement or for other alien purposes. Any signs of exploitative intentions in the behavior of the sponsor would also be expected to operate as negative incentives, evoking responses that conflict with the positive incentive value of improvising arguments in support of the conclusion assigned by the sponsor. *Thus, incentive theory predicts that role playing will be more successful in inducing attitude change if the sponsor is perceived as someone whose affiliations are benign in character and whose intentions are to promote public welfare than if he is perceived as someone whose affiliations and purposes are commercial or exploitative* (p. 18) [italics ours].

To test this prediction, subjects were asked to write essays favoring a year of required physics and mathematics for all college students. Half of them (favorable sponsorship) were told that the request originated from a national research organization conducting a survey for a number of leading universities. The other half (unfavorable sponsorship) were told that the sponsor was a commercial publisher who would use the information in a science textbook sales campaign. Within each sponsorship condition, half the subjects were offered $20 for writing the essay and half were offered $1. Payment of the monetary reward preceded the essay writing.

Control groups consisted of four additional conditions in which subjects received the same

81

sponsorship and monetary information; however, these groups did not engage in counterattitudinal encoding. Instead, control subjects merely committed themselves to write the essay, after which the attitude measures were taken. Incentive theory holds that this situation should produce minimal attitude change (Janis, 1968).

Although the sponsorship prediction is straightforward, Janis and Gilmore assert the probable effects of varied monetary payment are ambiguous: as we indicated earlier, if a large payment is perceived as justifiable, its positive incentive value will facilitate attitude change; if the payment is so large that it excites suspicion, it will serve as a negative incentive inhibiting attitude change. Since postexperimental interviews revealed mixed subject perceptions of the $20 payment, Janis and Gilmore's findings pertaining to monetary justification are inconclusive.

Among subjects participating in counterattitudinal advocacy, Janis and Gilmore found significantly more attitude change in the favorable-sponsorship conditions, a finding consistent with incentive theory and apparently at odds with dissonance predictions. This effect was not observed among control subjects, who agreed to participate in overt counterattitudinal encoding but did not actually do so.

Elms and Janis (1965), although dealing with the same variables as Janis and Gilmore, sought to sharpen their manipulations to test more conclusively a predicted interaction between attractiveness of sponsor and amount of monetary payment. They predict that, when paired with a favorable sponsor, a large monetary payment will serve as a positive incentive facilitating attitude change, whereas with an unfavorable sponsor, a large payment will function negatively thus inhibiting self-persuasion.

Subjects wrote essays supporting a jointly sponsored United States and Soviet program to send qualified American students to study in the Soviet Union for four years. A pretest revealed that subjects were opposed to this proposal; thus the requested encoding task was clearly counterattitudinal. Favorable-sponsorship subjects were told that the essays were for a survey research firm contracted by the State Department to assess American student attitudes toward the program and that the essays were to be used in preparing a pamphlet, detailing both sides of the issue, which would be read by all students surveyed in the study. By contrast, un-favorable-sponsorship subjects were led to believe that the experimenter represented a firm contracted by the Soviet Embassy to gather arguments for a pamphlet presenting arguments favoring the proposal. Subjects were told the pamphlet would be distributed to all American college campuses.

Since Janis and Gilmore found that the $20 reward aroused some suspicion, Elms and Janis pretested several amounts to determine a plausible large reward. On the basis of pretest results, the large monetary payment was set at $10 and the small payment at $0.50. Subjects were paid before the counterattitudinal essays were written.

Results generally supported the incentive theory prediction of an interaction between sponsorship and monetary payment. Among subjects actually encoding counterattitudinal essays, significantly greater attitude change occurred in the favorable-sponsorship conditions, a replication of Janis and Gilmore's finding. Most of this effect can be attributed to subjects in the favorable-sponsorship–large-payment condition, who reported significantly more change than subjects in any other condition.

Elms and Janis do, however, report one disquieting finding. Since positive incentives supposedly facilitate invention and improvisation of arguments, favorable-sponsorship subjects should encode higher quality essays. Whereas the earlier work of Janis and Gilmore supports this assumption, there is no evidence of differential quality between the conditions of Elms and Janis. Thus support for the biased scanning interpretation of incentive theory effects is at best equivocal.

What does the research on the effects of justification have to offer the persuasion practitioner? Un-questionably, the conflicting findings of various studies make it impossible to offer sovereign generalizations. Several studies dealing with monetary justification support the inverse relationship between justification and self-persuasion posited by dissonance theory; they suggest that the persuader should provide minimal justification for counterattitudinal advocacy. On the other hand, most of the sponsorship research conforms with the incentive theory prediction of a direct relation between justification and self-persuasion; it implies the persuader should employ high justification. How are these apparently contradictory claims to be reconciled?

First, it should be emphasized that monetary justification and justification based on type of sponsorship differ in several important respects. In particular, it is usually easier to assess the effects of a particular sponsor than of a particular amount of money. Given an attractive sponsor, negative incentives should not be activated by his request. But as we indicated earlier, it is often difficult to determine the value attached by an individual to a given sum of money. What may strike the persuader as a just salary may be seen by the persuadee as a contemptible bribe. Thus, unless one is quite certain of the financial attitudes of the intended persuadee, it may be safer to manipulate justification by means of sponsorship. Moreover, the ambiguity surrounding monetary justification creates interpretive problems when dealing with much of the relevant research literature.

Second, the studies discussed previously have perhaps oversimplified the problem. Instead of considering the single variable of justification, it may be more useful to examine the ways that justification relates to or interacts with other variables. Such an approach might cause us to invoke the qualifying phrase, "it depends": *in some cases, low justification might result in greater self-persuasion, whereas in others, high justification might have greater persuasive impact.* With this thought in mind, we turn next to several studies that have examined the relation of justification to other variables.

THE RELATIONSHIP OF JUSTIFICATION TO OTHER VARIABLES

Carlsmith, Collins, and Helmreich (1966) were among the first to study the effects of other variables on justification in a counterattitudinal advocacy situation. These researchers reasoned that if a situation involves face-to-face counterattitudinal advocacy—a high degree of public commitment—justification will be negatively related to self-persuasion, but if counterattitudinal essays are written anonymously—a low degree of public commitment—the relation between the two variables will be positive. The results obtained supported this reasoning.

In a later study, Linder, Cooper, and Jones (1967) predicted an interaction between magnitude of justification and amount of decision freedom: if an individual has considerable choice about engaging in counterattitudinal advocacy, low justification will result in greater self-persuasion; if choice is minimal, high justification will produce greater modification of initial attitudes. Again, the results conformed with predictions.

The findings of these studies, as well as others (e.g., Helmreich & Collins, 1968; Nel, Helmreich, & Aronson, 1969) indicate that it is possible to accommodate apparently conflicting claims about the role of justification in counterattitudinal advocacy if situational factors are carefully specified. In particular, the studies suggest that both dissonance and incentive theories correctly predict the relation between justification and subsequent self-persuasion, but only under certain encoding circumstances.

Miller and McGraw (1969) dealt with the possibility that high or low justification may be differentially effective in producing self-persuasion, depending on the point in time at which the persuasive measure is obtained. Recall that in Chapter 4 we asserted that the dissonance interpretation requires only *commitment to encode* counterattitudinally for self-persuasion to occur, whereas the incentive position requires *actual encoding*. Consistent with this distinction, Miller and McGraw hypothesized that in instances involving only commitment to encode, persons given low justification for encoding will demonstrate greater self-persuasion; conversely, following actual counterattitudinal encoding, persons given high justification will report greater attitude change.

Attitudes of subjects provided high or low justification for engaging in counterattitudinal advocacy were measured twice: first following commitment to encode counterattitudinal messages and second following message encoding. The results strongly supported the hypothesized dissonance effect at the commitment level. Low-justification subjects who agreed to encode a counterattitudinal essay favoring a lottery draft system changed from strong opposition to moderate support of the policy. High-justification subjects also reported a significant commitment change; however, it was significantly lower than the change reported by low-justification subjects. The unexpected commitment change by high-justification subjects may have occurred because of an ineffective manipulation of high justification or because of covert encoding behaviors (rehearsal) on the part of these subjects (Janis & Gilmore, 1965).

Unfortunately, the postencoding measures did not support the hypothesized superiority of high justification; in fact, the amount of change from commitment through postencoding was negligible for both conditions. Apparently, attitudes toward the belief-discrepant issue stabilized following commitment to encode, with actual encoding having little or no subsequent impact. Since one of Miller and Mc-Graw's possible explanations for this nonsignificant finding touches on a problem of central import to incentive theory, it is worth stating here:

Incentive theory holds that increases in justification lead to more biased positive scanning of formerly negative arguments [which] . . . in turn leads to greater self-persuasion. It may well be, then, that a necessary condition for confirming incentive theory predictions is the use of subjects who are cognitively familiar with a number of relevant arguments about the particular issue. In the present study, it appeared that most subjects, while reporting strong affective reactions to a lottery draft system, were not acquainted with many arguments for or against such a system. For the most part, the written essays emphasized one or two very general arguments relating to the universal "fairness" of a lottery system. Thus, the circumstances surrounding encoding of belief-discrepant messages may have militated against incentive-based self-persuasion. While admittedly speculative, this possibility could be tested by using groups of subjects who differ in their initial familiarity with the message topic (p. 450).

In essence, the argument is as follows: if persons are to engage in open-minded consideration of belief-discrepant arguments, such arguments must be cognitively available. Frequently, because of unfamiliarity with the issue or selective exposure to information, individuals may have trouble generating the needed arguments. Thus, if a persuader takes the incentive approach and provides a persuadee with high justification for engaging in counterattitudinal advocacy, he should be certain the persuadee is acquainted with some belief-discrepant arguments. If he has any doubts, the persuader might use the "pump priming" technique of Janis and Gilmore (1965); that is, he might provide the persuadee with some written cues to remind him of certain arguments.

We have only sampled results from studies investigating the relation of justification to other variables. These experiments convey a note of caution to those who would use counterattitudinal advocacy as a persuasive strategy. Like any persuasive transaction, counterattitudinal advocacy is complex, and justification is only one of numerous variables that may influence persuasive outcomes. Unless the persuader weighs these variables carefully, he will meet with less than ideal persuasive success. To return to our hypothetical example, it isn't easy to be a father, particularly a persuasive one.

choice

As we indicated in Chapter 4, all the major theoretical interpretations of counterattitudinal advocacy effects seem to imply that choice and self-persuasion are positively related: if the advocate feels he has a choice about encoding, he should change his attitudes or behaviors more than if he perceives that choice is lacking. Still, when attempts are made to examine the effects of choice in a research setting, several problems are readily apparent. An early study by Cohen and Latane (Brehm & Cohen, 1962) illustrates one of them.

Subjects were asked to tape record counterattitudinal speeches favoring a compulsory religion course at Yale University. Low-choice subjects were arbitrarily requested to give the speeches:

"The microphone was practically pushed into their hands, and they were given no choice to decline or to have any say in the matter" (p. 89). By contrast, high-choice subjects were exposed to the following induction:

"We need some people to speak in favor of the proposal, but, of course, the matter is entirely up to you." In effect, the experimenter attempted to create the illusion that the subject was entirely free to refuse, at the same time that the *experimenter reopened the issue* (of the subject's participating by giving a speech in favor of the proposal) every time the *subject appeared to be vacillating and on the edge of refusal.* In this manner the *experimenter and the subject sometimes "argued" back and forth as much as three times, but in all cases agreement was finally reached. Furthermore, after agreement was reached, the experimenter emphasized that he did not want to force the subject into anything he did not want to do,* and he made certain the decision was again seen by the subject as his own decision (p. 89) [italics ours].

From the perspective of the subject, it stretches credulity to label these circumstances *high choice.* He is told that the matter is entirely up to him, but each time he is on the verge of refusing—admittedly, sometimes as often as three times—the experimenter again urges him to perform the counterattitudinal task. Moreover, in every instance, the subject eventually agrees to engage in counterattitudinal advocacy. Since the concept of choice implies the existence of viable alternatives, procedures that rely on repeated pleas for cooperation and yield unanimity of action fall considerably short of the mark. Certainly, the entire undertaking would be more convincing if a few subjects had refused to participate.

In fairness to Cohen and Latane, we should note that their results support the predicted relation between choice and postencoding attitude change: high-choice subjects demonstrated significantly greater self-persuasion than their low-choice counterparts. Moreover, several other investigators (e.g., Brock, 1962; Linder, Cooper, & Jones, 1967; Holmes & Strickland, 1970) have found that subjects given high choice manifest more self-persuasion than low-choice subjects. Therefore, we are not questioning the likelihood that the two variables are positively related, nor are we suggesting that previous manipulations of choice have been total failures. Instead, we are only underscoring an obvious dilemma. If the promise of choice is nothing more than a token offering, the variable has not been manipulated effectively. On the other hand, if protestations of choice are perceived as sincere, a high refusal rate seems to be inevitable, since most people will be reluctant to engage in counterattitudinal advocacy.

For example, Bodaken (1970) pretested a high-choice induction by showing the counterattitudinal encoding request to a number of undergraduate students and asking them how they would respond. Without exception, the students indicated that the choice was easy: they would refuse to comply. "On the basis of these reactions, the choice inductions were rewritten to include a sponsor (the Department of Communication) and some clarification of the bogus research project. It was reasoned that the addition of these elements would make it more difficult for experimental subjects to refuse" (p. 36). Thus the realities of the research situation caused Bodaken to modify his high-choice induction. Unfortunately, the added elements produced a manipulation that was less effective than desired.

Not only is effective manipulation of the choice variable difficult, it is undoubtedly an oversimplification to speak of *a* choice; rather, participation in a research project usually implies a series of choices. Holmes and Strickland (1970) demonstrated this:

In general, the varying approximations to "choice" are troublesome, in part because few subjects fail to volunteer. For example, in some experiments (e.g., Linder, Cooper, & Jones, 1967; Rosenberg, 1965) a subject appears alone for an appointment, often for a course credit and perhaps at some inconvenience; thus, there may be commitment effects already operating; he is met with a statement about a delay in the experiment's start; he is given access by the "psychologist" to a constructive way to fill the waiting period (and even an unspecified financial bonus to boot); he is then directed to another experiment, and there "allowed" to volunteer or not. A choice between waiting 20 (probably) unproductive minutes or taking part in another experiment may induce negative compliance pressures (Linder *et al.*, 1967, p. 250) by reducing the freedom not to comply. *One cannot be sure when the critical choice occurs or, indeed, how many have been made* (pp. 39–40) [*italics ours*].

Not only does each decision reduce the impact of the choice manipulation—that is, commitment to participate may already be so firm that the attempt to induce high choice is of little consequence—it also clouds interpretation of findings obtained under differing experimental procedures.

The importance of these problems is not limited to the research arena; they are equally relevant to the persuasion practitioner. Although our hypothetical father may wish to give his son considerable freedom of action, he is likely to realize that if he does, the son will refuse to encode the anti-marijuana message. How is he to cope with this dilemma? Apparently, the best course available (and admittedly, it is far from satisfactory) is for the father to do everything possible to maximize his son's perceptions of decision freedom, while at the same time structuring the situation so that refusal is difficult. Obviously, this is a fine psychological line to walk.

Earlier we mentioned that Bem's self-perception theory provides an alternative explanation of certain counterattitudinal advocacy effects originally attributed to dissonance arousal. Probably the most interesting test of the two positions is found in a recent experiment by Bem and McConnell (1970), which utilized the choice variable. In this study, subjects were given either high or low choice about engaging in counterattitudinal advocacy. All subjects then encoded a counterattitudinal message, and afterward half of them were asked to report their postencoding attitudes toward the initially belief-discrepant issue. The other half, however, were not requested to report postencoding attitudes; rather, their task was to recall their original attitudes. Bem and McConnell reasoned that if the dissonance interpretation is correct, high-choice subjects should recall their initial attitudes accurately. On the other hand, if they used their message-encoding behaviors to infer their existing attitudes, as self-perception theory posits, it should be difficult for high-choice subjects to recall their original attitudes.

Results of a manipulation check indicated clear

differences in perceptions of choice between subjects in the choice and no-choice conditions. Moreover, for subjects reporting postencoding attitudes, the expected dissonance effect was obtained. Choice condition subjects demonstrated significantly greater attitude change in the direction of the belief-discrepant position than did no-choice and control subjects. The latter two groups did not differ significantly.

But what of the critical research question: do subjects remember their initial attitudes? A measure of accuracy was derived by subtracting each subject's initial attitude from his postencoding recall of that attitude. The attitude recall results turned out to be remarkably similar to the attitude change findings. On the 61-interval scale used to measure both attitude change and attitude recall, subjects in the choice treatment made an average recall error of 9.7 units. No-choice subjects' average error was 3.2 units, and control subjects erred one unit. All errors were in the direction of the belief-discrepant position.

As a second test of the question, subjects in the attitude recall experiment were asked to report their postencoding attitudes *after* they had attempted to recall their initial attitudes. For both the choice and no-choice groups, the correlation between recall and postencoding attitudes was significantly higher than the correlation between recall and actual initial attitudes. For control subjects, the correlations were in the opposite direction, but they did not differ significantly.

As a whole, then, it appears that although control subjects were fairly successful in recalling initial attitudes, subjects in the experimental groups—particularly the choice condition—did not remember so well. Bem and McConnell (1970) interpret the attitude-recall results in this way:

The figures are so similar to those in Table 1 [the attitude change figures] that it would appear that we had asked these subjects for their current attitudes rather than their initial attitudes. This is the pattern of results anticipated by the self-perception analysis of the forced-compliance experiment: actual premanipulation attitudes are not salient features of postmanipulation phenomenology and are recalled as identical to postmanipulation attitudes (p. 28).

We hasten to add that although the results of this study establish self-perception theory as a viable contender in the counterattitudinal advocacy arena, they do not rule out the dissonance interpretation. Bem and McConnell themselves admit that the results are readily interpretable within a dissonance framework. For if subjects do change their attitudes to reduce dissonance generated by discrepancy between their prior beliefs and their public behaviors, forgetting the initial, conflicting attitude may be an integral part of the dissonance reduction process. Whether present methods provide a means for determining which process is at work is exceedingly doubtful.

Perhaps our discussion of choice has muddied rather than cleared the persuasive waters. Certainly choice is a perplexing variable for the persuader who wishes to employ counterattitudinal advocacy—its relative presence or absence undoubtedly affects persuasive outcomes, but its effective manipulation poses a thorny challenge. Still, by understanding the relation of choice to self-persuasion, the sensitive persuader may find it possible to structure the situation in ways calculated to increase perceived choice, and hence persuasive impact. At least, the potential rewards justify the effort, a variable to which we now turn.

effort

As we have stated, both dissonance and incentive theory recognize the importance of effort in the counterattitudinal advocacy process. Dissonance theory holds that effort and self-persuasion are directly related: the greater the effort, the greater the dissonance and subsequent pressure for attitude change. For the incentive theorist, effort is inextricably bound up with justification, since positive incentives supposedly motivate persons to work harder at composing belief-discrepant arguments. Self-perception theory has not yet dealt directly with the effort variable; however, high effort expenditure should increase the probability that an individual will infer that his attitudes are accurately reflected by his encoding behavior. Therefore, for

92

all theoretical interpretations, it seems to be safe to conclude that high effort should facilitate self-persuasion.

Despite the apparent significance of the variable, few studies have dealt with the effects of effort on attitude change following counterattitudinal advocacy. Moreover, the methods typically used to render effort operational seem to be somewhat removed from "real-life" persuasive situations. Thus Zimbardo (1965) varied effort by asking subjects to read counterattitudinal arguments under differing conditions of delayed auditory feedback. In the high-effort condition, the delay interval (0.3 seconds) produced speech disruption and made comprehension difficult. The delay interval (0.01 seconds) used in the low-effort condition did not create severe problems.

Although Zimbardo's dissonance-derived hypothesis of a positive relation between effort and self-persuasion was supported, it is obvious that a persuasion practitioner will seldom have the opportunity to rig up persuadees in a delayed sidetone apparatus. Still, the persuader may find it possible to control the physical conditions under which counterattitudinal advocacy occurs. For example, our hypothetical father could ask his son to present an anti-marijuana message in a noise-filled, distraction-laden setting, the assumption being that such a setting would demand greater encoding effort.

Rather than manipulating effort, Blum and Wright (1964) had subjects assign themselves to high-effort and low-effort conditions. Subjects had 20 minutes to write counterattitudinal essays dealing with the issue of censorship. After completing their essays, all subjects filled out the posttest attitude measure; in addition, they rated the degree of effort they had expended writing the essays. Those who said they had expended considerable effort were placed in the high-effort group; those who reported low effort expenditure were assigned to the low-effort condition.

Results supported the hypothesized positive relation between effort and subsequent self-persuasion. Once again, however, the method used to vary effort has severe practical limitations. For the persuasion practitioner, success hinges on assuring high effort expenditure *before the fact* of counter-

Table 2 Effort differential paradigm

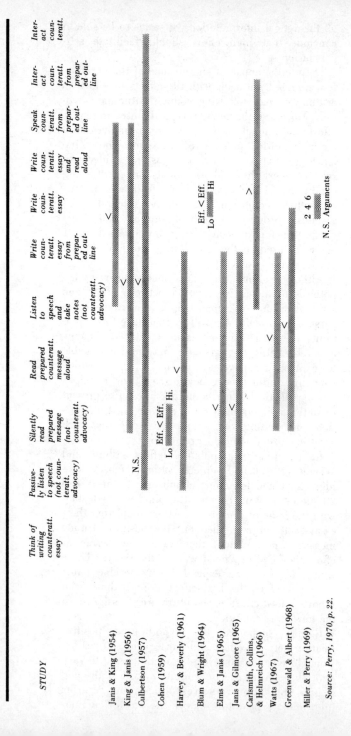

Source: Perry, 1970, p. 22.

attitudinal encoding. To check *after the fact* is of
little consequence, for if the persuadee has not
exerted himself, there is not much that can be done
about it at that point—unless, of course, the persuader can induce the persuadee to encode another
message.

Perhaps the best potential approach to varying
effort in actual persuasive situations is found in
Perry's (1970) effort differential paradigm. Her
paradigm, summarized in abbreviated form in
Table 2, identifies two potential sources of differential effort: 1 / the extent of the advocate's cognitive
involvement in counterattitudinal encoding, and
2 / the degree of physical and social proximity
existing between the counterattitudinal advocate
and the ostensible target audience. As Table 2
indicates, minimum effort should be expended in
situations requiring a low degree of cognitive involvement by the counterattitudinal advocate;
however, maximum effort should be exerted when
cognitive involvement is high and when the advocate and his ostensible target audience are engaged
in face-to-face interaction.

Columns on the left side of Table 2 indicate low-
effort conditions; those on the right are indicative
of high energy output. In addition, studies that
have varied the type of encoding situation are
summarized, and the direction of the caret indicates
the condition in which greater attitude change
occurred. With only one or two exceptions, the
studies support the assumption that more persuasion takes place under conditions of highly effortful
encoding. Perry argues that in the maximal effort
situation, "the advocate must argue energetically
and become more interested in his task of improvising new arguments and restating points than in
any of the previous conditions" (pp. 24–25). Moreover, "each plateau of this paradigm . . . requires
more involvement, more energy, and more effort
than the previous plateau" (p. 25).

Whether Perry has correctly ordered the various
encoding situations in terms of their effort-produc-
ing potential is itself an unanswered empirical
question. It is interesting to note that previous
research findings generally conform with the
ordering. Moreover, the practical advantages of her
approach are quickly apparent. Although it may be

difficult for a persuader to set up an experiment utilizing a delayed sidetone apparatus or a noisy room, some control of the conditions under which messages are prepared or the audience settings in which they are delivered is usually possible. If our hypothetical father can involve his son in a heated argument with a dissenting peer about the evils of marijuana, he is likely to have greater success than if the son writes an essay for an ostensible audience that is not even physically present.

For the persuader seeking maximum impact, a little effort is, undoubtedly, a dangerous thing. As we have emphasized, the key problem involves effective manipulation of the effort variable. Perry's approach appears to offer one promising avenue. The resourceful persuader can probably identify other options that will do the job, options that will demand maximum effort from the counterattitudinal advocate.

initial audience attitudes

Recall the controversy between "early" and "later" dissonance interpretations of counterattitudinal advocacy effects, spelled out in Chapter 4. At its heart is the issue of the influence of initial audience attitudes: for the "early" dissonance advocate, initial audience attitudes are essentially irrelevant; for the proponent of "later" dissonance theory, they are a crucial determinant of dissonance arousal and subsequent self-persuasion. In this section, we consider representative research bearing on the "early"–"later" dissonance controversy, as well as two of our own studies designed to test predictions derived from "later" dissonance theorizing.

Nel, Helmreich, and Aronson (1969) varied monetary justification ($0.50 vs. $5) and initial audience attitudes (opposed, in favor, no opinion). They hypothesized that: 1 / Counterattitudinal advocates addressing an uncommitted audience will report greater self-persuasion under conditions of low justification than under conditions of high justification. 2 / Greatest self-persuasion will occur in the uncommitted audience condition. 3 / There will be a positive relation between justification and self-persuasion in the condition where the audience favors the position advocated.

Support for the hypotheses was at best equivocal. The original analysis yielded no significant differences, but a secondary comparison revealed a significant difference between high- and low-justification subjects who encoded for an uncommitted audience. This difference was consistent with theoretical expectations (i.e., subjects receiving low justification reported significantly greater self-persuasion than did high-justification subjects).

Cooper and Worchel (1970) provided more substantial support for the aversive consequences viewpoint championed by "later" dissonance theorists. Subjects engaged in a modified replication of the Festinger and Carlsmith study described earlier in this chapter. Half the subjects in both the high- and low-justification conditions were told that they had been successful in convincing the supposedly naïve subject that the dull task was actually interesting, whereas the other half were told that they had been unsuccessful. All subjects then reevaluated the dull task. As predicted, only those subjects who complied for low monetary payment and who were led to believe they had deceived the supposedly naïve subject came to believe the task was interesting. Although initial audience attitude was not manipulated in this study, the findings are consistent with the assumption that an uncommited audience is more likely to suffer the aversive consequence of being persuaded to accept a position at odds with the advocate's beliefs. Cooper and Worchel provided the following interpretation of their results:

The data of the present experiment clearly point to the importance of considering the consequences of role-playing behavior in the induction of cognitive dissonance. According to Festinger and Carlsmith's original formulation of the theory, opinion change should have been evidenced when counterattitudinal advocacy was performed for minimal incentive. The present experiment has shown that counterattitudinal advocacy per se has little effect on a person's opinion. Rather, opinion change occurs only when an attitude-discrepant speech that had been made for a small incentive results in consequences that are undesirable (p. 204).

Bodaken and Miller (1971) manipulated the variables of choice and initial audience attitude.

Subjects were given high or low choice about writing a counterattitudinal essay arguing that college undergraduates should be required to live on campus. Half the subjects were told that their ostensible target audience was undecided on this issue, whereas the other half were told the audience already favored the proposal. Although there was no significant effect for the choice variable, the audience results clearly supported the "later" dissonance interpretation; that is, subjects who encoded for the uncommitted audience reported significantly greater self-persuasion than did subjects whose essays were aimed at committed readers.

The preceding evidence is by no means overwhelming, but there are certainly grounds for arguing that an uncommitted audience increases the persuasive impact of counterattitudinal advoccacy. Even if some doubt remains, however, the persuasion practitioner would be well advised to arrange the situation so that the persuadee believes that he is communicating with an uncommitted audience. If the "early" dissonance interpretation eventually proves to be more tenable, such a strategy can do no harm; and should "later" dissonance theory prevail, an uncommitted audience would be a definite persuasive asset.

We have previously stated that all individuals are not likely to be equally susceptible to the moral misgivings central to the "later" dissonance interpretation of counterattitudinal advocacy. For instance, persons who habitually manipulate others out of considerations of self-interest should experience few moral qualms when encoding to an uncommitted audience, particularly if they are amply rewarded for their counterattitudinal communication.

To test this possibility, Burgoon, Miller, and Tubbs (1972) conducted a study in which high and low Machiavellians (Christie & Geis, 1970) encoded counterattitudinal essays for an uncommitted audience under conditions of high or low justification. Since high Machiavellians are not averse to manipulating others, they should experience less dissonance than their low-Machiavellian counterparts when communicating to a highly persuasible audience for minimally justifying reasons. Conversely, when considerable justification is offered, high Machiavellians should associate only positive incentives with the encoding task, whereas low Machiavellians should perceive the potentially persuasive audience as a negative incentive. Taken as a whole, these considerations led to the following hypothesized interaction: when counterattitudinal messages are prepared for an uncommitted audience under conditions of low justification, low Machiavellians will report significantly greater self-persuasion than highs; but when messages are prepared under conditions of high justification, high Machiavellians will report significantly greater self-persuasion than lows.

The results strongly supported the hypothesis; in fact, differences between high and low Machiavellians were exactly as predicted and were, in all cases, significant. Thus, in cases involving high-Machiavellian persuadees, a persuader is likely to find the "later" dissonance approach, with its emphasis on morality and ethics, to be of limited utility. Instead, the persuader should proffer ample justification for engaging in counterattitudinal advocacy, a tactic calculated to heighten positive incentives for high-Machiavellian advocates. Gauging relative Machiavellianism is, of course, yet another difficult challenge the persuader faces.

Not only do specific characteristics of the counterattitudinal advocate influence self-persuasion predictions derived from "later" dissonance theorizing, but differences in audience makeup may also exert a powerful impact on dissonance arousal. Widgery and Miller (1972) hypothesized that advocates encoding for a familiar, uncommitted audience would report more self-persuasion than advocates encoding for an audience of uncommitted strangers. There were two reasons for this prediction: first, advocates should experience greater concern about possible aversive consequences occurring for friends or acquaintances than for strangers; second, in terms of self-concept, those advocates communicating counterattitudinally with friends or acquaintances should deem it more probable that the audience will know their actual attitudes, and hence will perceive them as liars or hypocrites. Results confirmed the hypothesis; by far the most self-persuasion occurred among those subjects who encoded for an uncommitted, familiar audience.

Researchers have just begun to study the many persuader and persuadee factors that may influence dissonance arousal in situations involving counter-attitudinal advocacy. As work continues, some rather complex relationships will undoubtedly be unearthed. Despite this complexity, however, the resourceful persuader who grasps the workings of a few key variables achieves a definite persuasive advantage. We cannot guarantee our hypothetical father's persuasive success, but we believe that he can improve his chances if he understands the research summarized in the preceding pages.

when is a counterattitudinal message really counterattitudinal? a note of caution

Almost all the findings discussed in this chapter rest on one key assumption: *if a persuadee agrees to engage in counterattitudinal advocacy, he will encode a message that is clearly counterattitudinal.* This assumption is obviously open to question, for persons may accept a counterattitudinal task and still compose an uncommitted, or a belief-congruent message. Such inconsistency between assent and action may occur consciously, because of the negative consequences associated with counterattitudinal advocacy, or unconsciously, because of the notorious unreliability of human perception. Moreover, to the extent that the advocate is able to avoid actual counterattitudinal commitment, minimal self-persuasion effects would be anticipated.

Research by Burgoon (1970) and Burgoon and Miller (1971) sheds further light on this problem. In both studies, it was found that many of those who agreed to engage in counterattitudinal encoding actually prepared messages that were not clearly counterattitudinal. Furthermore—and this finding is of crucial import to the persuasion practitioner— self-persuasion occurred only when the advocate encoded an intensely counterattitudinal message. The lesson seems clear: mere compliance with the request for counterattitudinal encoding does not guarantee a belief-discrepant product, and such a product is essential for subsequent self-persuasion. Burgoon and Miller suggest some strategies that increase the likelihood of a clearly counterattitudinal message, but the onus of responsibility in an actual persuasive situation falls heavily on the persuader. Not only must he induce the persuadee to perform the counterattitudinal task, he must also structure the encoding situation to ensure belief-discrepant output. If he fails in the latter undertaking, all his persuasive efforts probably will have gone for naught.

---

summing up

In this chapter we have reviewed a number of studies dealing with variables influencing the persuasive impact of counterattitudinal advocacy. Although here we have only scratched the surface, it should be apparent that variables such as justification, choice, effort, and initial audience attitude deserve careful scrutiny by students of persuasion and persuasion practitioners alike. Both theoretical understanding and practical persuasive success hinge on these and other similar factors. This quest for understanding and success is an exciting one, and it has only just begun.

THE APPLICATION
OF NEW PERSUASIVE
TECHNIQUES: SOME
CONCLUDING THOUGHTS

Our discussion of the new persuasive techniques of counterattitudinal advocacy, role playing, and methods for inducing resistance to persuasion is ended. Although we share a dislike for lengthy epilogues, some brief comments about the application of these techniques seem to be warranted. Most of the questions raised below have evolved from dialogues with concerned students and colleagues. There are no "right" answers, unlike many of the research queries posed earlier in this volume. Our own thoughts concerning them are, at best, tentative and speculative. Still, since the issues involved warrant the attention of all serious students of persuasion, we set forth our current thinking here.

the relevance of these
new persuasive techniques

Often, after waxing enthusiastically about the new techniques of persuasion discussed in this book, we have encountered some variation of the following skeptical charge: "What you've said is all very interesting, but it's also very impractical. The kinds of things you've been talking about seldom, if ever, go on outside the research laboratory."

We reject this charge emphatically. The most cursory examination of the institutions of later twentieth century American society reveals the persuasive influence of such techniques as role playing and counterattitudinal advocacy—even though they may not always be used with persuasive intent. What student has not, at one time or another, encoded counterattitudinally in the classroom? What parent has never asked his or her child to verbalize reasons why a certain behavior was inappropriate? Who in business and industry has not been exposed to the intricacies of participative decision making? For that matter, what reader cannot recall instances when he came to believe something because he had been behaving *as if* he believed it? All these examples do not necessarily represent pure instances of role playing or counterattitudinal advocacy; it should be obvious, however, that these persuasive processes contribute heavily to any attitudinal or behavioral changes that may occur.

One reservation should be noted. As we indicated earlier, we feel that considerably more attention has been devoted to persuasive techniques aimed at bringing about change than has been directed at methods designed to inhibit change. Perhaps in our dynamic, change-oriented society this bias is inevitable. Nevertheless, in a culture saturated with persuasive communication, any semblance of permanence or stability rests on making some values, attitudes, and behaviors relatively resistant to change. Surely, some features of our society are worth preserving, even though there may be those among us who call stridently for their demise. Unless we understand ways of inducing resistance to change, a gullible populace may prove to be an easy mark for the unscrupulous persuasive huckster.

Not only are these new techniques of persuasion an integral part of contemporary society, we suspect that they are more effective than traditional approaches to influence—although admittedly we now have little data to support our hunch. Still, if any term captures the flavor of today's life style, it is the term *involvement*. People spurn the role of passive onlooker; they search for ways to become involved, experiencing participants in the events that swirl around them. Techniques such as role playing and counterattitudinal advocacy capitalize on this desire for involvement; they make the persuadee a central, active participant in the influence process. After all, what better way to satisfy the craving for involvement than to allow the persuadee the psychological luxury of persuading himself?

Nothing we have said is intended to sound the death knell for those more traditional approaches to influence, which have long been the object of study by students of persuasion. Unquestionably, these tried and proven strategies will continue to occupy an important place in the arsenal of persuasive weapons. As we stressed in Chapter 1, the techniques described here are intended to augment the traditional persuasive approaches, not to replace them. The one modest claim we make is that these new techniques are relevant to contemporary society, and as such, they deserve the attention of both the persuasion practitioner and the persuasion researcher.

the ethics of these new persuasive techniques

Ethical questions have always been closely linked with the persuasive process. Each time an individual asks the factual question "How can I persuade?" he has some obligation to ponder the concomitant value query "Is it ethical for me to employ this particular means of persuasion?" Unquestionably, there are many who will seriously doubt the ethical propriety of such persuasive techniques as role playing and counterattitudinal advocacy, particularly since these approaches often require the intended persuadee to make public utterances that are initially at odds with his private beliefs.

Some of our acquaintances have gone so far as to issue a blanket indictment against any persuasive technique that relies on public falsehood. Under no circumstances, say these critics, is such an approach justified. This position seems to us to be unduly rigid and unrealistic. As we have already pointed out, a great deal of counterattitudinal advocacy takes place in our society. In fact, we have observed with amusement that several of the critics who subscribe to this position are notorious for their conformity demands in the classroom. Of course, if confronted with this charge, these persons would deny any malicious motivation or persuasive intent; in such cases, the student is only being held to the rational, intelligent viewpoint. Despite such protestations, we detect a potential inconsistency, for if requests for belief-discrepant public behavior are always unethical, the student should be free to espouse whatever position he chooses with no fear of negative consequences. In short, we believe that it is impossible to eliminate all instances of counterattitudinal advocacy from our society, and even if it could be done, we are not at all certain it would be a good thing.

Others have suggested that some instances of persuasion resulting from counterattitudinal advocacy are ethically defensible, but others are not. One acquaintance has argued that if self-persuasion conforms to the incentive model, with its emphasis on open-minded consideration of formerly belief-discrepant arguments, then the persuader is on morally sound grounds. On the other hand, if self-persuasion results only from thoughtless pressures for private and public consistency—the keystone of the dissonance interpretation—then the persuader has been ethically remiss.

This argument may have some validity, but it rests on the questionable assumption that the persuader is capable of identifying the precise mediating circumstances that led to an observed persuasive effect. If behaviorial scientists are unable to agree on the best explanation for certain scientific findings —and as we have indicated throughout this volume, there is considerable disagreement among those researchers interested in interpreting counterattitudinal advocacy effects—it is doubtful that the persuasion practitioner will be able to specify exactly what happened, even though his influence attempt may be successful. Given these explanatory shortcomings, most persuaders will naturally argue that their persuasive efforts conform with some rational, ideal model of persuasion and that persuadees change because of careful examination of the belief-discrepant arguments, not because of blind, irrational behavior.

In the absence of any clear answers to this ethical issue, we are forced to conclude that each potential persuader must define the moral limits of role playing, counterattitudinal advocacy, or for that matter, any other persuasive technique at his disposal. Our major goal in this volume has been description, not prescription. If anyone wishes to summarily dismiss all these techniques as unethical, this is certainly his prerogative. Conversely, if others feel that ethical questions are irrelevant (i.e., if they define persuasion as an amoral process), they will view this whole discussion as pointless. Although we do not subscribe to either of these extreme positions, we recognize that ethics is an intensely personal matter. We can identify situations in which we would feel perfectly justified in using these persuasive techniques and others in which we would not. We trust that the reader can make the same decision.

Finally, some may question the ethics of our entire undertaking on the grounds that the techniques described in this book extend man's possibilities of controlling his fellow men. We do not necessarily share this aversion to control, however, and we will content ourselves with pointing out the other side of the persuasive coin. *If knowledge can be used to exert control, it can also be used to resist control.* As we observed in Chapter 1, these techniques of persuasion have been employed for some time; they are "new" only in the sense that researchers have recently embarked on systematic attempts to study and to understand them. Any knowledge gained from these attempts benefits the potential persuadee, as well as the persuader. If our hypothetical son reads this volume, all his father's persuasive blandishments probably will be to no avail. Perhaps this is a comforting thought with which to conclude.

REFERENCES

ABELSON, R. P., & ROSENBERG, M. J. Symbolic psychologic: A model of attitudinal cognition. *Behavioral Science*, 1958, *3*, 1–13.

ARONSON, E. Dissonance theory: Progress and problems. In R. P. Abelson et al. (eds.), *Theories of Cognitive Consistency: A Sourcebook.* Chicago: Rand McNally, 1968, pp. 5–27.

BARON, R. M. Attitude change through discrepant action: A functional analysis. In A. G. Greenwald, T. C. Brock, & T. M. Ostrom (eds.), *Psychological Foundations of Attitude.* New York: Academic Press, 1968, pp. 297–326.

BEM, D. J. An experimental analysis of self-persuasion. *Journal of Experimental Social Psychology,* 1965, *1*, 199–218.

BEM, D. J. Attitudes as self-descriptions: Another look at the attitudes–behavior link. In A. G. Greenwald, T. C. Brock, & T. M. Ostrom (eds.), *Psychological Foundations of Attitude.* New York: Academic Press, 1968, pp. 197–215.

BEM, D. J., & McCONNELL, H. K. Testing the self-perception explanation of dissonance phenomena: On the salience of premanipulation attitudes. *Journal of Personality and Social Psychology,* 1970, *14*, 23–31.

BENNETT, E. Discussion, decision, commitment and consensus in "group decisions." *Human Relations,* 1955, *8,* 251–274.

BERGER, C. R. The effects of influence feedback and need influence on the relationship between incentive magnitude and attitude change. *Speech Monographs,* 1969, *36,* 435–442.

BERGER, C. R. When inconsistency is fun: Toward a dramaturgic theory of attitude change. Unpublished manuscript, School of Speech, Northwestern University, 1971.

BETTINGHAUS, E. P. *Persuasive Communication.* New York: Holt, Rinehart & Winston, 1968.

BLUM, M., & WRIGHT, J. M. Degree of effort and attitude change under forced compliance. *Psychonomic Science,* 1964, *1,* 67–68.

BODAKEN, E. M. Choice and perceived audience attitudes as determinants of cognitive dissonance and subsequent attitude change following counterattitudinal advocacy. Unpublished doctoral dissertation, Department of Communication, Michigan State University, 1970.

BODAKEN, E. M., & MILLER, G. R. Choice and prior audience attitude as determinants of attitude change following counterattitudinal advocacy. *Speech Monographs,* 1971, *38,* 107–112.

BREHM, J. W., & COHEN, A. R. *Explorations in Cognitive Dissonance.* New York: John Wiley & Sons, 1962.

BREMBECK, W. L., & HOWELL, W. S. *Persuasion.* Englewood Cliffs, N. J.: Prentice-Hall, 1952.

BROCK, T. C. Cognitive restructuring and attitude change. *Journal of Abnormal and Social Psychology,* 1962, *64,* 264–271.

BURGOON, M. Ability of individuals to judge the positions taken in belief-congruent and belief-discrepant messages. Unpublished manuscript, Department of Communication, Michigan State University, 1970.

BURGOON, M., & MILLER, G. R. Prior attitude and language intensity as predictors of message style and attitude change following counterattitudinal advocacy. *Journal of Personality and Social Psychology,* 1971, *20,* 246–253.

BURGOON, M., MILLER, G. R., & TUBBS, S. L. Machiavellianism, justification, and attitude change following counterattitudinal advocacy. *Journal of Personality and Social Psychology*, 1972, *22*, 366–371.

CARLSMITH, J. M. Varieties of counterattitudinal behavior. In R. P. Abelson et al. (eds.), *Theories of Cognitive Consistency: A Sourcebook*. Chicago: Rand McNally, 1968, pp. 803–809.

CARLSMITH, J. M., COLLINS, B. E., & HELMREICH, R. K. Studies in forced compliance: I. The effect of pressure for compliance on attitude change produced by face-to-face role playing and anonymous essay writing. *Journal of Personality and Social Psychology*, 1966, *4*, 1–13.

CHRISTIE, R., & GEIS, F. L. *Studies in Machiavellianism*. New York: Academic Press, 1970.

COOPER, J., & WORCHEL, S. Role of undesired consequences in arousing cognitive dissonance. *Journal of Personality and Social Psychology*, 1970, *16*, 199–206.

CRONKHITE, G. *Persuasion: Speech and Behavioral Change*. Indianapolis: Bobbs-Merrill, 1969.

CRUTCHFIELD, R. S. Conformity and character. *American Psychologist*, 1955, *10*, 191–198.

ELMS, A. C. *Role Playing, Reward, and Attitude Change*. New York: Van Nostrand-Reinhold Company, 1969.

ELMS, A. C., & JANIS, I. L. Counter norm attitudes induced by consonant versus dissonant conditions of role playing. *Journal of Experimental Research in Personality*, 1965, *1*, 50–60.

FESTINGER, L. *A Theory of Cognitive Dissonance*. Evanston, Ill.: Row, Peterson, 1957.

FESTINGER, L., & CARLSMITH, J. M. Cognitive consequences of forced compliance. *Journal of Abnormal and Social Psychology*, 1959, *58*, 203–210.

FISHER, S., RUBINSTEIN, I., & FREEMAN, R. W. Intertrial effects of immediate self-committal in a continuous social influence situation. *Journal of Abnormal and Social Psychology*, 1956, *52*, 200–207.

FORER, B. R. Therapeutic relationships in groups. In A. Burton (ed.), *Encounter*. San Francisco: Jossey-Bass, 1969, pp. 27–41.

GELFAND, D. M. The influence of self-esteem on the rate of verbal conditioning and social matching behavior. *Journal of Abnormal and Social Psychology*, 1962, *65*, 259–265.

GOLLOB, H. G., & DITTES, J. E. Different effects of manipulated self-esteem on persuasibility depending on the threat and complexity of the communication. *Journal of Personality and Social Psychology*, 1965, *2*, 195–201.

HEIDER, F. *The Psychology of Interpersonal Relations.* New York: John Wiley & Sons, 1958.

HELMREICH, R. K., & COLLINS, B. E. Studies in forced compliance: Commitment and magnitude of inducement to comply as determinants of opinion change. *Journal of Personality and Social Psychology*, 1968, *10*, 75–81.

HOCHBAUM, G. M. The relation between group members' self-confidence and their reactions to group pressures to uniformity. *American Sociological Review*, 1954, *19*, 678–687.

HOLMES, J. G., & STRICKLAND, L. H. Choice freedom and confirmation of incentive expectancy as determinants of attitude change. *Journal of Personality and Social Psychology*, 1970, *14*, 39–45.

JANIS, I. L. Attitude change via role playing. In R. P. Abelson et al. (eds.), *Theories of Cognitive Consistency: A Sourcebook.* Chicago: Rand McNally, 1968, pp. 810–818.

JANIS, I. L., & FESHBACH, S. Effects of fear-arousing communications. *Journal of Abnormal and Social Psychology*, 1953, *48*, 78–92.

JANIS, I. L., & GILMORE, J. B. The influence of incentive conditions on the success of role playing in modifying attitudes. *Journal of Personality and Social Psychology*, 1965, *1*, 17–27.

JANIS, I. L., & MANN, L. Effectiveness of emotional role-playing in modifying smoking habits and attitudes. *Journal of Experimental Research in Personality*, 1965, *1*, 84–90.

KELLEY, H. H. Attribution theory in social psychology. *Nebraska Symposium on Motivation*, 1967, *15*, 192–238.

KELMAN, H. C. Effects of success and failure on "suggestibility" in the autokinetic situation. *Journal of Abnormal and Social Psychology*, 1950, *45*, 267–285.

KELMAN, H. C. et al. Studies in attitude-discrepant behavior. Unpublished manuscript, Department of Psychology, Harvard University, 1969.

KELMAN, H. C., & HOVLAND, C. I. "Reinstatement" of the communicator in delayed measurement of opinion change. *Journal of Abnormal and Social Psychology*, 1953, *48*, 327–335.

KEUTZER, C. S., LICHTENSTEIN, E., & HIMES, K. H. "Emotional" role playing and changes in smoking attitudes and behavior. *Proceedings*, 77th Annual Convention, APA, 1969, 373–374.

KIESLER, C. A. Commitment. In R. P. Abelson et al. (eds.), *Theories of Cognitive Consistency: A Sourcebook*. Chicago: Rand McNally, 1968, pp. 448–463.

KIESLER, C. A. *The Psychology of Commitment: Experiments Linking Behavior to Belief*. New York: Academic Press, 1971.

KIESLER, C. A., & SAKUMURA, J. A test of a model for commitment. *Journal of Personality and Social Psychology*, 1966, *3*, 458–467.

LEWIN, K. *Field Theory in Social Science*. New York: Harper & Row, 1951.

LEWIN, K. Group decision and social change. In G. Swanson, T. Newcomb, & E. Hartley (eds.), *Readings in Social Psychology*. New York: Holt, Rinehart & Winston, 1958, pp. 197–212.

LEWIN, K. Group decision and social change. In H. Proshansky & B. Seidenberg (eds.), *Basic Studies in Social Psychology*. New York: Holt, Rinehart & Winston, 1965, pp. 423–437.

LINDER, D. E., COOPER, J., & JONES, E. Decision freedom as a determinant of the role of incentive magnitude in attitude change. *Journal of Personality and Social Psychology*, 1967, *6*, 245–254.

MACAULAY, J. R. A study of independent and additive modes of producing resistance to persuasion derived from congruity and inoculation models. Unpublished doctoral dissertation, Department of Psychology, University of Wisconsin, 1965.

MANN, L. The effects of emotional role playing on desire to modify smoking habits. *Journal of Experimental Social Psychology*, 1967, *3*, 334–348.

MANN, L., & JANIS, I. L. A follow-up study on the long-term effects of emotional role playing. *Journal of Personality and Social Psychology*, 1968, *8*, 339–342.

MAUSNER, B., & BLOCH, B. A study of the additivity of variables affecting social interaction. *Journal of Abnormal and Social Psychology*, 1957, *54*, 250–256.

McGUIRE, W. J. Resistance to persuasion conferred by active and passive prior refutation of the same and alternative counterarguments. *Journal of Abnormal and Social Psychology*, 1961, *63*, 326–332.

McGUIRE, W. J. Persistence of the resistance to persuasion induced by various types of prior belief defenses. *Journal of Abnormal and Social Psychology*, 1962, *64*, 241–248.

McGUIRE, W. J. Inducing resistance to persuasion: Some contemporary approaches. In L. Berkowitz (ed.), *Advances in Experimental Social Psychology*, Vol. 1. New York: Academic Press, 1964, pp. 191–229.

McGUIRE, W. J. The nature of attitudes and attitude change. In G. Lindzey & E. Aronson (eds.), *The Handbook of Social Psychology*, Vol. 3. Reading, Mass.: Addison-Wesley, 1969, pp. 136–314.

McGUIRE, W. J., & PAPAGEORGIS, D. The relative efficacy of various types of prior belief-defense in producing immunity against persuasion. *Journal of Abnormal and Social Psychology*, 1961, *62*, 327–337.

McGUIRE, W. J., & PAPAGEORGIS, D. Effectiveness of forewarning in developing resistance to persuasion. *Public Opinion Quarterly*, 1962, *26*, 24–34.

MILLER, G. R. Saying is believing: Toward a rhetoric of counterattitudinal advocacy. Unpublished manuscript, Department of Communication, Michigan State University, 1969.

MILLER, G. R. Counterattitudinal advocacy: A current appraisal. In C. D. Mortensen & K. K. Sereno (eds.), *Advances in Communication Research*. New York: Harper & Row, 1972.

MILLER, G. R., & McGRAW, R. L. Justification and self-persuasion following commitment to encode, and actual encoding of counterattitudinal communication. *Speech Monographs*, 1969, *36*, 443–451.

MILLMAN, S. The relationship between anxiety, learning, and opinion change. Unpublished doctoral dissertation, Department of Psychology, Columbia University, 1965.

MORENO, J. L. The psychodrama. In J. E. Fairchild (ed.), *Personal Problems and Psychological Frontiers*. New York: Sheridan House, 1957, pp. 276–285.

NEL, E., HELMREICH, R. K., & ARONSON, E. Opinion change in the advocate as a function of the persuasibility of his audience: A clarification of the meaning of dissonance. *Journal of Personality and Social Psychology*, 1969, *12*, 117–124.

NELSON, C. Anchoring to accepted values as a technique for immunizing beliefs against persuasion. Unpublished doctoral dissertation. Department of Psychology, Columbia University, 1966.

NEWCOMB, T. M. An approach to the study of communicative acts. *Psychological Review*, 1953, *60*, 393–404.

NUNNALLY, J., & BOBREN, H. Variables influencing the willingness to receive communications on mental health. *Journal of Personality*, 1959, *27*, 38–46.

OSGOOD, C. E., & TANNENBAUM, P. H. The principle of congruity in the prediction of attitude change. *Psychological Review*, 1955, *62*, 42–55.

PAPAGEORGIS, D. Anticipation of exposure to persuasive messages and belief change. *Journal of Personality and Social Psychology*, 1967, *5*, 490–496.

PERRY, B. L. The effort variable in counterattitudinal advocacy. Unpublished manuscript, Department of Communication, Michigan State University, 1970.

POLSTER, E. Encounter in community. In A. Burton (ed.), *Encounter*. San Francisco: Jossey-Bass, 1969, pp. 138–161.

ROKEACH, M., & ROTHMAN, G. The principle of belief congruence and the congruity principle as models of cognitive interaction. *Psychological Review*, 1965, *72*, 128–142.

ROSENBAUM, M. E., & FRANC, D. E. Opinion change as a function of external commitment and amount of discrepancy from the opinion of another. *Journal of Abnormal and Social Psychology*, 1960, *61*, 15–20.

ROSENBAUM, M. E., & ZIMMERMAN, I. M. The effect of external commitment on responses to an attempt to change opinions. *Public Opinion Quarterly*, 1959, *23*, 247–254.

ROSENBERG, M. J. When dissonance fails: On eliminating evaluation apprehension from attitudinal measurement. *Journal of Personality and Social Psychology*, 1965, *1*, 28–42.

SAMELSON, F. Conforming behavior under two conditions of conflict in the cognitive field. *Journal of Abnormal and Social Psychology*, 1957, *55*, 181–187.

SCHEIDEL, T. M. *Persuasive Speaking*. Glenview, Ill.: Scott, Foresman, 1967.

SINGER, R. P. The effects of fear-arousing communication on attitude change and behavior. Unpublished doctoral dissertation, Department of Psychology, University of Connecticut, 1965.

STUKÁT, K. G. *Suggestibility: A Factorial and Experimental Study*. Stockholm: Almqvist & Wiksell, 1958.

TANNENBAUM, P. H. Initial attitude toward source and concept as factors in attitude change through communication. *Public Opinion Quarterly*, 1956, *20*, 413–425.

TANNENBAUM, P. H. Mediated generalization of attitude change via the principle of congruity. *Journal of Personality and Social Psychology*, 1966, *3*, 493–499.

TANNENBAUM, P. H., MACAULAY, J. R., & NORRIS, E. L. Principle of congruity and reduction of persuasion. *Journal of Personality and Social Psychology*, 1966, *3*, 233–238.

TANNENBAUM, P. H., & NORRIS, E. L. Effects of combining congruity principle strategies for the reduction of persuasion. *Sociometry*, 1965, *28*, 145–147.

WARD, S., & WACKMAN, D. Family and media influences on adolescent consumer learning. *American Behavioral Scientist*, 1971, *14*, 415–427.

WEISS, W., & FINE, B. J. The effect of induced aggressiveness on opinion change. *Journal of Abnormal and Social Psychology*, 1956, *52*, 109–114.

WIDGERY, R. N., & MILLER, G. R. Audience familiarity and prior audience attitude as determinants of attitude change following counterattitudinal advocacy. *Proceedings*, 80th Annual Convention, APA, 1972, 147–148.

ZIMBARDO, P. G. The effect of effort and improvisation on self-persuasion produced by role playing. *Journal of Experimental Social Psychology*, 1965, *1*, 103–120.

INDEX OF NAMES

INDEX OF SUBJECTS